ROOTES

of the 1950s, 1960s & 1970s

Hillman, Humber, Singer, Sunbeam & Talbot

A Pictorial History
David Rowe

VELOCE

CONTENTS

For full model listing, see the Index.

Rootes: a brief history

The founders of the Rootes Group, William (Billy) and Reginald Rootes were born in Hawkhurst, Kent, where their father William (senior) had a cycle shop. As his business grew, William decided to set up a motor agency selling, amongst others, Hillman and Humber cars. When he left school Billy joined Singer Motors in Coventry as an apprentice, but subsequently took on a role running a new branch of his father's business. Reginald initially had no interest in the motor trade, but later joined his brother and together – with financial help from their father – they set up Rootes Ltd in Maidstone. Their next step was to set up a distribution business with a showroom in London, and they also acquired control of Thrupp and Maberly – a coachbuilding company. In 1926 the pair moved their offices and showroom into newly built premises, Devonshire House, Piccadilly. Billy had become interested in taking over companies that manufactured cars, to fit in with owning a coachbuilding

Humber military vehicles.

The report on the Volkswagen V.W.82 (Beetle).

Top: The author's first car – a Hillman Minx, registration 233 TKX. Bottom left: His second car – a Hillman Super Minx, registration 724 SYA. Bottom right: His third Rootes car – a Hillman Minx deluxe, registration PFR 9H.

company and distributing cars, and the chance came when William Hillman and Thomas Humber both found themselves experiencing financial problems, thus providing the Rootes brothers with the opportunity of acquiring a stake in both companies in 1929. Between 1934 and 1938, Rootes acquired commercial vehicle manufacturers Karrier, British Light Steel Pressings (not the Pressed Steel company), Sunbeam, Talbot and finally Singer in December 1955. The Rootes Group took advantage of the Government's Shadow factory scheme, introduced in anticipation of the second World War, and built aircraft, armoured vehicles and, of course, Field Marshal Montgomery's Humber staff car. Perhaps, had it not dismissed the opportunity of producing the Volkswagen Beetle when the war ended, we would now be driving the Hillman Golf or Humber Passat, and the Rootes group would be a major international company. Unfortunately, during the 1960s, a lengthy strike by workers who supplied parts to Rootes factories, the costs involved in getting the Imp into production, and possibly the decision to continue with the Minx and Gazelle alongside the Super Minx and Vogue at a time when car sales were generally falling, led the Rootes Group into financial difficulty, and ultimately into the hands of Chrysler and subsequently Peugeot. It is also interesting to speculate on what might have happened if Alexander Issigonis, designer of the Morris Minor and Mini, had remained at Humber where he was briefly employed in the late 1920s, or if the husbands of William Hillman's daughters, John Black of Standard Triumph and Spencer Wilks, who joined Rover and inspired the Land Rover, had remained with the Hillman company, where they were both employed as directors.

Hillman Minx mark 4

The Minx mark 4 was introduced in 1949 to replace the 1948 mark 3, which itself had been the first of a new generation of updated and completely restyled Hillmans without the separate front wings associated with 1930s cars, but the mark 3 had retained the 1185cc engine from its predecessors. The mark 4 now featured an enlarged engine of 1265cc; also new were sturdier front bumpers, which gave the impression they wrapped further around the car, and separate front sidelights, but otherwise there was nothing to distinguish it from the mark 3. The Minx name had been used by Hillman on a number of cars since 1932. Mechanical improvements included the introduction of a counter-balanced crankshaft and water pump bolted to the front of the cylinder block. A passenger sun visor was still optional.

COLOURS (1949): Embassy black, Dove grey, Pastel green, Pastel blue.
ENGINE: Four-cylinder, SV, bore 65mm, stroke 95mm, 1265cc, maximum bhp 37.5 at 4200rpm, Solex 30FAI downdraught carburettor.
GEARBOX: Four-speed, steering column gear change, synchromesh on top three gears. Ratios: top 5.22:1, 3rd 7.78:1, 2nd 12.9:1, 1st 18.6:1, reverse 24.84:1.
REAR AXLE: Semi-floating, spiral bevel, ratio 5.22:1.
Note: increase in engine size over phase 3 from 1185cc to 1265cc, achieved by increasing bore from 63mm to 65mm.
BRAKES: Lockheed, front and rear 8in drums.
TYRES: Saloon 5.00 x 16, estate 5.00 x 15.
SUSPENSION: Front coil springs, rear semi-elliptic leaf springs.
STEERING: Burman worm and nut variable ratio.
DIMENSIONS: Length: saloon/convertible 13ft 1.25in (3994mm), estate 13ft 8in (4166mm); **width:** 5ft 2in (1575mm); **height:** saloon 5ft 0in (1524mm), convertible 4ft 10.5in (1486mm), estate 5ft 5.75in (1670mm); **turning circle:** 33ft (10m).
CAPACITIES: Fuel 7.25 gallons (33 litres). Boot 11ft³ (0.3m³).

Steering column gear change layout.

Hillman Minx mark 5

Introduced in 1951, vertical chrome strips either side of the front grille, and side trim on the front doors and wings differentiated the mark 5 from the mark 4. It retained the same engine capacity, but now came with revised pistons. This tweaking of the engine would remain a feature of the Minx in the years that followed, with later modifications to cylinder head and manifolds. Revised steering and a longer gear change lever were also introduced with the mark 5. Optional extras: heater, radio, overriders, and more.

COLOURS (1952): Mid green, Quartz blue, Claret, Nimbus grey, Embassy black.
ENGINE: Four-cylinder, SV, bore 65mm, stroke 95mm, 1265cc, maximum bhp 37.5 at 4200rpm, Solex 30FAI downdraught carburettor.
GEARBOX: Four-speed, steering column gear change, synchromesh on top three gears. Ratios: top 5.22:1, 3rd 7.78:1, 2nd 12.9:1, 1st 18.6:1, reverse 24.84:1.
REAR AXLE: Semi-floating, spiral bevel, ratio 5.22:1.
BRAKES: Lockheed, front and rear 8in drums.
TYRES: Saloon 5.00 x 16, estate 5.00 x 15.
SUSPENSION: Front coil springs, rear semi-elliptic leaf springs.
STEERING: Burman worm and peg variable ratio.
DIMENSIONS: Length: saloon/convertible 13ft 1.25in (3994mm), estate 13ft 8in (4166mm); **width:** 5ft 2in (1575mm); **height:** saloon 5ft 0in (1524mm), convertible 4ft 10.5in (1486mm), estate 5ft 5.75in (1670mm); **turning circle:** 33ft (10m).
CAPACITIES: Fuel 7.25 gallons (33 litres). Boot 11ft³ (0.3m³).

Non-standard amber indicators have been fitted to the mark 5 models above, and the black car has been featured in a number of magazine articles and also the television programme 'Back in Time for Dinner.'

Instrument layout.

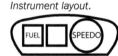

Hillman Minx mark 6
'Anniversary' model

Produced for only eight months in 1953, it retained the same body with 'short' boot as the mark 5, but had different rear lights and the revised frontal treatment and technical specification of the mark 7. Optional extras included heater, radio, overriders, rim finishers, and more.

This mark 6 was left outside whilst its owner spent years restoring a mark 5.

Hillman Minx mark 7

Introduced in 1953, appearing identical to the mark 6 from the front and also having the revised dashboard that was introduced with the mark 6, the mark 7 was 2in longer, featured a revised rear end with enlarged rear window, and had, according to the brochure, a 10% bigger boot. Optional extras: heater, radio, overriders, rim finishers, and more.

COLOURS (1953): Saloon/convertible: Embassy black, Mid green, Quartz blue, Claret, Golden sand, Mountain grey. Estate: Cruiser grey, Golden sand, Smoke blue. Californian (first is main body colour, second is roof): Cream/Black, Pastel green/Bottle green, Balmoral grey/Quartz blue, Cream/Pippin red.
ENGINE: Four-cylinder, SV, bore 65mm, stroke 95mm, 1265cc, maximum bhp 37.5 at 4200rpm, Solex 30FAI downdraught carburettor (later cars Zenith 30VM7).
GEARBOX: Four-speed, steering column gear change, synchromesh on top three gears. Ratios: top 5.22:1, 3rd 7.78:1, 2nd 12.89:1, 1st 16.64:1, reverse 21.07:1.
REAR AXLE: Semi-floating, spiral bevel, ratio 5.22:1.
BRAKES: Lockheed, front and rear 8in drums.
TYRES: Saloon 5.00 x 16, estate 5.50 x 15.
SUSPENSION: Front coil springs, rear semi-elliptic leaf springs, Armstrong shock absorbers all round.
STEERING: Burman worm and peg variable ratio.
DIMENSIONS: Length: 13ft 3.25in (4045mm); **width:** 5ft 3.5in (1613mm); **height:** saloon 5ft 0in (1524mm); **weight:** saloon 18cwt 3qtr 21lb (962kg); **turning circle:** 33ft (10m).
CAPACITIES: Fuel 7.25 gallons (33 litres).

Rear light arrangements:
A: Minx mark 3, 4, 5
B: Minx mark 6
C: Minx mark 7, 8, 8a

A B C

Hillman Minx mark 8

Introduced in 1954, the mark 8 range comprised the Deluxe saloon, Special saloon, Californian coupé, estate and convertible. Externally the Special saloon lacks the side chrome strip, and neither the Special or estate models have the rear wing stone guards that appear on the cars featured here. Neither did they have the new OHV engine introduced with the mark 8, which would remain in production for 25 years, although it would ultimately 'grow' to 1725cc. All models, however, featured the larger boot and revised rear end introduced with the mark 7.

COLOURS: All saloons: included Embassy black, Mountain grey, Pearl grey, Mid green, Olive green, Golden beige, Magnolia, April yellow. Deluxe saloon only: Corinth blue, Claret. Estate: Elephant grey, Smoke blue. Convertible: Embassy black, Mountain grey, Corinth blue, Mid green, Magnolia, Claret.
ENGINE: Deluxe saloon, convertible and Californian coupé only: Four-cylinder, OHV, bore 76.2mm, stroke 76.2mm, 1390cc, maximum bhp 43 at 4400rpm, Zenith 30VI downdraught carburettor.
GEARBOX: Four-speed, steering column gear change, synchromesh on top three gears. Ratios: top 4.78:1, 3rd 7.13:1, 2nd 11.81:1, 1st 17.05:1, reverse 22.73:1.
REAR AXLE: Semi-floating, spiral bevel, ratio 4.78:1.
ENGINE: Estate and 'Special' saloon only:

Four-cylinder, SV, bore 65mm, stroke 95mm, 1265cc, maximum bhp 37.5 at 4200rpm, Zenith 30VM7 downdraught carburettor.
GEARBOX: Four-speed, steering column gear change, synchromesh on top three gears. Ratios: top 5.22:1, 3rd 7.78:1, 2nd 12.89:1, 1st 18.6:1, reverse 24.851.
REAR AXLE: Semi-floating, spiral bevel, ratio 5.22:1.
BRAKES: Lockheed, front and rear 8in drums.
TYRES: Saloon 5.60 x 15, estate 5.50 x 15.
SUSPENSION: Front coil springs and wishbones, rear semi-elliptic leaf springs, Armstrong shock absorbers all round.
STEERING: Burman worm and peg variable ratio.

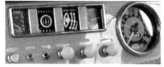

Instrument layout. Note: gear change diagram was included unless optional clock was fitted.

Steering column gear change layout.

DIMENSIONS: Length: saloon/coupé/convertible 13ft 3.25in (4045mm), estate 13ft 8in (4166mm); **width:** 5ft 3.5in (1613mm); **height:** saloon 5ft 1in (1549mm), coupé/convertible 5ft 0in (1524mm), estate 5ft 7.5in (1715mm); **weight:** Deluxe saloon 18cwt 3qtr 21lb (962kg), Special saloon 18cwt 1qtr (927kg); **turning circle:** 33ft (10m).
CAPACITIES: Fuel 7.25 gallons (33 litres).

The black convertible above has been fitted with non-standard amber front and rear indicators. See the other cars on this page for the standard indicator arrangement.

Hillman Minx mark 8a

Introduced in 1955 with new 'Gay Look' two-tone paintwork option, the mark 8a was the last of this particular style of Minx. It was also the end of the SV engine, with all models now using the OHV unit, with bhp up to 47 at 4400rpm. For detailed information on engine, gears, brakes, suspension, steering and dimensions/weight, see mark 8 on preceding page. Optional extras: heater, radio, overriders, whitewall tyres, rim finishers, two-tone paint finish (all models except special saloon); saloon: passenger sun visor (standard on Deluxe), and more.

COLOURS (1955): Deluxe saloon: two-tone, lower body colour first, Summer blue/Pearl grey, Pearl grey/Olive green, April yellow/Pearl grey, Corinth blue/Thistle grey. Single tones (all saloons), Embassy black, Golden beige, Corinth blue, Thistle grey, Cactus green. Estate: two-tone, lower body colour first, Elephant grey/Mist grey, Golden beige/Pearl grey, Elephant grey/Pearl grey. Californian: main body colour first, Summer blue/Pearl grey, Magnolia/Embassy black, Tyrolean green/Forest green, Magnolia/Pippin red, Embassy black/Pippin red, Oxford blue/Magnolia. Convertible: Embassy black, Thistle grey, Magnolia, Burgundy, Tyrolean green.

The boot lid for the car above has been restyled to accommodate the new two-tone paint finish introduced with the mark 8a (see mark 8 cars on previous pages for comparison).

Hillman Minx series 1

Introduced in 1956, the series 1 was an all-new design, and part of a whole family of new, similarly-styled Rootes cars, the others badged as the Singer Gazelle and Sunbeam Rapier, introduced in 1955. The spare wheel was now in an upright position in the boot instead of a separate compartment under the boot floor; all pedals were now pendant

Front grilles: Top left, mark 4; top right, mark 5; lower left, marks 6 & 7; lower right, marks 8 & 8a.

The green car above has had circular chrome trims added to the front wings.

Pedal arrangements: mark Minx on left; series Minx on right.

Spare wheel stowage: mark Minx on left; series Minx on right.

type instead of being on the floor, but the handbrake remained by the right-hand side of the driver's seat, and warning lights were now in a binnacle on the steering column. The Minx was available as a Deluxe or Special saloon, convertible, and, from 1957, an estate. Alexander Engineering produced a high performance version of the Minx with twin SU carburettors, raised engine compression ratio, enlarged inlet ports and Laycock overdrive, it was identified by a wide side-flash. Optional extras: heater, radio, clock, oil pressure gauge, ammeter, overriders, whitewall tyres, rim finishers, two-tone paint and more.

COLOURS (1956): Deluxe saloon: two-tone, lower body colour first, Seacrest green/Pearl grey, April yellow/Pearl grey, Antelope/Pearl grey, Lilac grey/Storm grey. Single tones (all saloons), Embassy black, Corinth blue, Lilac grey, Antelope.

ENGINE: Four-cylinder, OHV, bore 76.2mm, stroke 76.2mm, 1390cc, maximum bhp 51 at 4400rpm, Zenith 30VI downdraught carburettor.

GEARBOX: Four-speed, steering column gear change, synchromesh on top three gears. Ratios: saloon top 4.78:1, 3rd 7.13:1, 2nd 11.81:1, 1st 17.05:1, reverse 22.73:1; estate top 5.22:1, 3rd 7.79:1, 2nd 12.89:1, 1st 18.6:1, reverse 24.85:1.

REAR AXLE: Semi-floating, spiral bevel, ratio: saloon 4.78:1, estate 5.22:1.

BRAKES: Lockheed 8in front and rear drums.

TYRES: Saloon 5.60 x 15.

SUSPENSION: Front coil springs and wishbones, rear semi-elliptic leaf springs, Girling telescopic shock absorbers all round.

STEERING: Burman worm and nut.

DIMENSIONS: Length: 13ft 4.5in (4077mm); **width:** 5ft 0.75in (1542mm); **height:** saloon 4ft 11.5in (1511mm), convertible 4ft 10in (1473mm), estate 5ft 1in (1549mm); **weight:** Deluxe saloon 19cwt 2qtr 16lb (998kg), convertible 19cwt 3qtr 8lb (1007kg); **turning circle:** 36ft (11m).

CAPACITIES: Fuel 7.25 gallons (33 litres).

Hillman Minx series 2

Introduced in 1957 to replace the series 1, and known as the Jubilee model because it celebrated 25 years of the Hillman Minx name. Series 1 to 3 cars all shared the same body style, the apparent increase in length over the series 1 was simply the result of increasing the space between the bumpers and bodywork to reduce the potential for damage to the bodywork. Mechanically, it was unchanged from the series 1 introduced in 1956. A variation of the series 2 Minx was produced in Japan using the Isuzu name. Optional extras now included Manumatic automatic transmission and individual front seats, as well as the usual items such as heater, radio, clock, oil pressure gauge, ammeter, overriders, whitewall tyres, wheel trims, rim finishers, and more.

COLOURS (1957): Deluxe saloon: two-tones, lower body colour first, Seacrest green/Pearl grey, Fiesta blue/Pearl grey, Charcoal/Oyster grey, Antelope/Pearl grey, Calypso red/Pearl grey. Single tones (all saloons), Embassy black, Fiesta blue, Thistle grey, Antelope. Convertible: Embassy black with Red hood, Thistle grey with Red hood, Fiesta blue with Blue hood, Seacrest green with Green hood, Pippin red with Red hood, all above except Pippin red available with Black hood.

Arrow indicates the hole in the middle of the front bumper of the car on the right for a starting handle, ideal when the battery is flat because you left the lights on overnight!

Instrument layout for Deluxe saloons. Note: diagram includes optional oil and ammeter gauges, and warning lights are in separate binnacle on steering column.

ENGINE: Four-cylinder, OHV, bore 76.2mm, stroke 76.2mm, 1390cc, maximum bhp 51 at 4400rpm, Zenith 30VM8 downdraught carburettor.

GEARBOX: Four-speed, steering column gear change, synchromesh on top three gears. Ratios: saloon/convertible, top 4.78:1, 3rd 7.13:1, 2nd 11.81:1, 1st 17.05:1, reverse

22.73:1; estate, top 5.22:1, 3rd 7.79:1, 2nd 12.89:1, 1st 18.6:1, reverse 24.85:1.

REAR AXLE: Semi-floating, spiral bevel, ratio: saloon 4.78:1, estate 5.22:1.

BRAKES: Lockheed 8in front and rear drums.

TYRES: Saloon 5.60 x 15.

SUSPENSION: Front coil springs and wishbones, rear semi-elliptic leaf springs, telescopic shock absorbers all round.

STEERING: Burman worm and nut.

DIMENSIONS: Length: 13ft 6in (4115mm); **width:** 5ft 0.75in (1542mm); **height:** saloon 4ft 11.5in (1511mm), convertible 4ft 10in (1473mm), estate 5ft 1in (1549mm); **weight:** Deluxe saloon 19cwt 2qtr 16lb (998kg), convertible 19cwt 3qtr 8lb (1007kg); **turning circle:** 36ft (11m).

CAPACITIES: Fuel 7.25 gallons (33 litres).

The saloon above is a Special with non-standard two-tone paint scheme. All others are Deluxe saloons with normal two-tone paint scheme.

Steering column gear change layout.

Convertibles had less trim than Deluxe saloons. Left: series 2 has no side trim; middle: series 3 has side trim but no trim along the top edge of the rear wing; right: series 3a has trim on sides and along the edge of rear wing but like the other convertibles only has a short section of trim underneath the front quarter lights.

15

Hillman Minx series 3

Introduced in 1958 to replace the series 2, the series 3 featured an enlarged engine of 1494cc, recirculating ball steering, new dashboard layout, revised style of two-tone paintwork and a rectangular, rather than square, number plate was now fitted to the rear. This was the last of the saloons and convertibles with this style of rear wings; however, the rear end styling of the estate cars would remain unchanged until it was discontinued in 1962, following the introduction of the Super Minx estate. Optional extras: heater, radio, clock, oil pressure gauge, ammeter, screen washers, individual front seats, automatic transmission, overriders, whitewall tyres, wheel trims, rim finishers, and more.

COLOURS (1958): Deluxe saloon: two-tones, lower body colour first, Seacrest green/ Foam grey, Ocean blue/Foam grey, Powder blue/Charcoal, Antelope/Foam grey, Calypso red/Foam grey, Foam grey/Charcoal. Single tones (all saloons): Embassy black, Ocean blue, Antelope, Powder blue, Foam grey, Seacrest green. Estate: (two-tone, main body colour first, second is side and rear window surrounds): Calypso red/Cloud white, Windsor blue/Cloud white, Cypress green/Cloud white, Cavalry beige/Pearl grey, Light gun/Pearl grey, Single tones, Windsor blue, Cavalry beige, Light gun. Convertible: Embassy black with Red hood, Ocean blue with Green hood, Pippin red with Black hood, Powder blue with Blue hood, Moonstone with Blue hood, all above available with black hood.

Instrument layout, Deluxe models: cars can be found with speedometer on right or left. For Special saloon layout see page 18.

ENGINE: Four-cylinder, OHV, bore 79mm, stroke 76.2mm, 1494cc, maximum bhp 52.5 at 4400rpm, Zenith 30VM8 downdraught carburettor.

GEARBOX: Four-speed, steering column gear change, synchromesh on top three gears. Ratios: saloon/convertible, top 4.55:1, 3rd 6.79:1, 2nd 11.23:1, 1st 14.52:1, reverse 18.37:1; estate, top 4.78:1, 3rd 7.13:1, 2nd 11.81:1, 1st 15.23, reverse 19.30:1.

REAR AXLE: Semi-floating, spiral bevel, ratio: saloon 4.55:1, estate 4.78:1.

BRAKES: Lockheed, front and rear 8in drums.

TYRES: Saloon/convertible 5.60 x 15, estate 5.50 x 15 or 5.90 x 15.

SUSPENSION: Front coil springs and wishbones, rear semi-elliptic leaf springs, telescopic shock absorbers all round.

STEERING: Burman recirculating ball.

DIMENSIONS: Length: 13ft 6in (4115mm); **width:** 5ft 0.75in (1542mm); **height:** saloon 4ft 11.5in (1511mm), convertible 4ft 10in (1473mm), estate 5ft 1in (1549mm); **weight:** Deluxe saloon 19cwt 3qtr 18lb (1012kg), Special saloon 19cwt 1qtr 24lb (989kg), convertible 1 ton 0qtr 8lb (1020kg), estate 1 ton 1cwt 0qtr 1lb (1029kg); **turning circle:** 36ft (11m).

CAPACITIES: Fuel 7.25 gallons (33 litres).

Steering column gear change layout on left, and floor gear change layout for Special saloon on right.

This series 3 estate has been repainted in a darker colour than the original red.

Hillman Minx series 3a/3b

The series 3a was introduced with newly restyled wrapover rear wings, a new front grille with rectangular sidelights, and larger 9in brakes (except the Special which retained 8in drums). In 1960 it was replaced by the identical looking 3b, which was fitted with a stainless steel front grille and hypoid bevel rear axle. Optional extras: heater, radio, clock, oil pressure gauge, ammeter, Easidrive automatic transmission replaced the earlier Manumatic, reversing light, overriders, rim finishers, two-tone paint scheme (some with matching two colour interior trim).

COLOURS (1959): Deluxe saloon: two-tone, lower body colour first, Ember red/Foam white, Ocean blue/Foam white, Charcoal/Powder blue, Antelope/Foam white, Apple green/Foam white, Caramel/Regency beige. Single tones (all saloons), Embassy black, Antelope, Ocean blue, Powder blue, Apple green, Foam white, Thistle grey. Estate: two-tone, main body colour first, second is side and rear window surround and side flash, Windsor blue/Foam white, Cypress green/Foam white, Ascot grey/Foam white, Calypso red/Foam white, Charcoal/Foam white. Single tones: Charcoal, Ascot grey, Windsor blue. Convertible: Main body colour first, second is side flash, Powder blue/Corinth blue with Corinth blue hood, Moonstone/Embassy black with black hood, Moonstone/Powder blue with Powder blue hood, Ocean blue/Foam white with Cypress green hood, Ember red/Embassy black with black hood, Embassy black/Pippin red with Pippin red hood, all above available with black hood.
ENGINE (3b): Four-cylinder, OHV, bore 79mm, stroke 76.2mm, 1494cc, maximum bhp

This estate has been fitted with 13in wheels, hence is lower to the ground than normal.

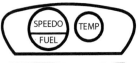

Instrument layout for Special saloon. See page 16 for Deluxe layout.

18

56.5 at 4600rpm, Zenith 30VN downdraught carburettor.

GEARBOX (3b): four-speed, floor-mounted gear change standard (steering column change optional), synchromesh on top three gears. Ratios: saloon/convertible, top 4.44:1, 3rd 6.19:1, 2nd 9.51:1, 1st 14.87:1, reverse 18.84:1; estate, top 4.86:1, 3rd 6.76:1, 2nd 10.40:1, 1st 16.25:1, reverse 20.59:1.

REAR AXLE (3b): Semi-floating, hypoid bevel, ratio: saloon/convertible 4.44:1, estate 4.86:1 (3a, spiral bevel, ratio: saloon/convertible 4.55, estate 4.78).

Left: standard floor gear change layout; right: optional steering column change.

BRAKES: Lockheed 9in front and rear drums.
TYRES: Saloon 5.60 x 15, estate 5.50 x 15 or 5.90 x 15.
SUSPENSION: Front coil springs and wishbones, rear semi-elliptic leaf springs, telescopic shock absorbers all round.
STEERING: Burman recirculating ball.
DIMENSIONS: Length: 13ft 6in (4115mm); **width:** 5ft 0.75in (1542mm); **height:** saloon 4ft 11.5in (1511mm), convertible 4ft 10in (1473mm), estate 5ft 1in (1549mm); **weight:** Deluxe saloon 19cwt 3qtr 25lb (1015kg), convertible 1 ton 15lb (1023kg), estate 1 ton 3qtr 11lb (1060kg); **turning circle:** 36ft (11m).
CAPACITIES: Fuel 7.25 gallons (33 litres).

Cars on opposite page are all 3a; those on this page are all series 3b.

Hillman Minx series 3c

Introduced in 1961 to replace the series 3b, the 3c had an enlarged engine of 1592cc. This was the last of the Minx with roll-over style rear wings, but by Rootes standards it had a lengthy life of over two years. The special saloon was no longer available, and the convertible and estate were discontinued in 1962 following the introduction of the Super Minx. Optional extras: heater, radio, clock, oil pressure gauge, ammeter, screen washers, headlamp flasher, remote control bonnet lock, seat belts, automatic transmission, power assisted brake kit, reversing light, fog and spotlights, overriders, door or wing mirrors, wheel trim discs or rim finishers, tow bar, roof or boot rack, rear window anti-condensation panel, locking petrol cap, and more.

COLOURS (1962): Deluxe saloon: two-tones, lower body colour first, Charcoal/Powder blue, Glen green/Foam white, Lake blue/Foam white, Venetian red/Foam white, Morocco brown/Regency beige. Single tones, Embassy black, Foam white, Lake blue, Glen green, Thistle

Convertibles and estates retained the same side trim as the series 3a/3b models but can be identified by a 1600 badge on the doors, the saloon now had a single trim strip along the side.

Rear light and wings for Minx. Left to right: series 1 and 2, series 3, series 3a to 3c, series 5 and 6.

grey. Convertible: Powder blue/Corinth blue hood, Moonstone/Powder blue hood, Glen green/Glen green hood, Pippin red/Pippin red hood, all above available with black hood.
ENGINE: Four-cylinder, OHV, bore 81.5mm, stroke 76.2mm, 1592cc, maximum bhp 56.5 at 4100rpm, Zenith 30VN downdraught carburettor.
GEARBOX: Four-speed, floor-mounted gear change, synchromesh on top three gears. Ratios: saloon, top 4.22:1, 3rd 5.88:1, 2nd 9.04:1, 1st 15.82:1, reverse 21.09:1.

Floor gear change layout.

REAR AXLE: Semi-floating, hypoid bevel, ratio saloon 4.22:1.
BRAKES: Lockheed 9in front and rear drums.
TYRES: 5.60 x 15.
SUSPENSION: Front coil springs and wishbones, rear semi-elliptic leaf springs, Armstrong shock absorbers all round.
STEERING: Burman recirculating ball.
DIMENSIONS: Length: 13ft 6in (4115mm); **width:** 5ft 0.75in (1542mm); **height:** saloon 4ft 11.5in (1511mm), convertible 4ft 10in (1473mm), estate 5ft 1in (1549mm); **weight:** Deluxe saloon 19cwt 3qtr 25lb (1015kg); **turning circle:** 36ft (11m).
CAPACITIES: Fuel 7.25 gallons (33 litres).

Unfortunately, the car in front of this estate could not be started, so it had to remain in the garage whilst the estate was photographed.

Hillman Minx series 5

The series 5 was introduced in 1963 to replace the series 3c. There was no series 4, as the car originally intended to replace the 3c was launched as a separate model – the Super Minx – and it was then decided to continue with the original smaller, but restyled, Minx. Gone was the curved rear window, and the rear wings reverted to an earlier, simpler, style. Improvements over the 3c included a larger fuel tank, individual front seats, all gauges now in front of driver, front disc brakes, elimination of all greasing points, optional automatic was now Borg-Warner instead of Smiths Easidrive, and, from late 1964, windscreen washers and an all synchromesh gearbox.

COLOURS (1963): Two-tone, main body colour first, Azure blue/Powder blue, Glen green/Foam white, Pippin red/Birch grey, Forest green/ Sage green, Morocco brown/Regency beige, Charcoal/Birch grey. Single tones, Embassy black, Foam white, Glen green, Birch grey, Thistle grey, Forest green, Azure blue.
ENGINE: Four-cylinder, OHV, bore 81.5mm, stroke 76.2mm, 1592cc, maximum bhp 56.5 at 4100rpm, Zenith 30VN carburettor, (later cars Solex 33PSEI).
GEARBOX: Four-speed, floor-mounted gear change, synchromesh on top three gears, (all synchromesh from late 1964). Ratios: top 3.89:1, 3rd 5.41:1, 2nd 8.32:1, 1st 14.57:1, reverse 19.42:1; with optional Borg-Warner automatic: top 3.89, 2nd 5.64, 1st 9.31, reverse 8.14.
REAR AXLE: Semi-floating, hypoid bevel, ratio 3.89:1.
BRAKES: Lockheed, front 10.3in discs, rear 9in drums.

Floor gear change layout early models; later models as series 6.

Instrument layout.

The only model available was a Saloon.

22

TYRES: 6.00 x 13.
SUSPENSION: Front coil springs and wishbones, rear semi-elliptic leaf springs, telescopic shock absorbers all round.

STEERING: Burman recirculating ball.
DIMENSIONS/CAPACITIES: As series 6, except **weight:** 19cwt 2qtr (991kg).

Hillman Minx series 6

Introduced in 1965, the series 6 featured an enlarged engine of 1725cc, the same as that found in the Super Minx mark 4, and also featured the all-synchromesh gearbox, introduced towards the end of series 5 production, and retained the same gear ratios, despite the fact that engine size had increased. Visually, it was identical to the series 5, and, like the series 5, was only available as a saloon. Standard equipment included screen washers, headlamp flasher, individual front seats, front disc brakes, and all-synchromesh gearbox. Optional extras: heater, radio, clock, oil pressure gauge, ammeter, Borg-Warner automatic transmission, reversing light, overriders, whitewall tyres, wheel trim discs, and more.

COLOURS (1965): Two-tone, main body colour first, second is roof. Bermuda blue/Artic white, Forest green/Willow green, Willow green/Forest green, Storm grey/Alabaster grey, Kingfisher blue/Embassy black, Artic white/Tartan red, Slate blue/Dawn mist, Alabaster grey/Forest green, Tartan red/Embassy black, Single tones, Artic white, Storm grey, Alabaster grey, Forest green, Tartan red, Willow green, Bermuda blue, Slate blue, Kingfisher blue.
COLOURS (1966): Single tones only, Embassy black, Polar white, Storm grey, Tartan red, Willow green, Bermuda blue.

ENGINE: Now with five bearing crankshaft instead of three, four-cylinder, OHV, bore 81.5mm, stroke 82.5mm, 1725cc, maximum bhp 62.5 at 4200rpm, Zenith 34IV carburettor.
GEARBOX: Four-speed, floor-mounted gear change, synchromesh on all forward gears. Ratios: top 3.89:1, 3rd 5.41:1, 2nd 8.32:1, 1st 13.04:1, reverse 13.88.
REAR AXLE: Semi-floating, hypoid bevel, ratio 3.89:1.

BRAKES: Lockheed, front 10.3in discs, rear 9in drums.
TYRES: 6.00 x 13.
SUSPENSION: Front coil springs and

Left: Floor gear change layout.
Right: Optional automatic.

wishbones, rear semi-elliptic leaf springs, telescopic shock absorbers all round.
STEERING: Burman recirculating ball.
DIMENSIONS: Length: 13ft 5.5in (4102mm); **width:** 5ft 0.75in (1542mm); **height:** 4ft 10in (1473mm); **weight:** 1 ton 23lb (1026kg); **turning circle:** 36ft (11m).
CAPACITIES: Fuel 10 gallons (45 litres). Boot 9.2ft^3 (0.3m^3).

Instrument layout.

Front grilles from Minx models.
Left: Top, series 1; centre, series 2; bottom, series 3. Right: Top, series 3a to 3c; bottom, series 5 & 6.

Hillman Minx (Arrow)

Introduced in 1967 and discontinued in 1970, this was the last Rootes car to carry the Minx name, and in true Minx fashion the handbrake remained by the right-hand side of the driver's seat, even though the Imp introduced in 1963 had its handbrake located between the front seats. It used the same bodyshell as the Hunter, but featured a 1494cc engine, unless automatic transmission was specified, in which case the Hunter 1725cc engine was fitted. However, it did not have the Hunter opening front quarter lights. With so little to visually differentiate it from the Hunter, or the Singer Gazelle and Vogue perhaps, it is understandable that the Minx simply became the Hunter deluxe in 1970. The Minx name would reappear briefly on two Talbot models, the Solara and Alpine, in 1984. Standard equipment included heater and fresh air ventilation, screen washers, headlamp flasher, and rear door childproof locks. Optional extras: radio, clock, oil gauge, ammeter, Borg-Warner automatic transmission, fog, spot and reversing lights, overriders, wheel trims, and more.

COLOURS (1967): Saloon: Storm grey, Holly green, Signal red, Polar white, Midnight blue,

Cars on the right are standard, not deluxe models, and can be identified by lack of deluxe model side and rear trim strip.

All saloons on this page are Deluxe models. Additional equipment included carpet instead of rubber floor covering, two-speed blower and centre console, etc. The red car belonged to the author – a 1969 Minx, registration PFR 9H, with his wife at the wheel.

Shore beige. Estate: Storm grey, Neptune green, Signal red, Polar white, Oxford blue, Shore beige.
ENGINE: Four-cylinder, OHV, bore 81.5mm, stroke 81.5mm, 1496cc, maximum bhp 64 at 4800rpm, Stromberg 150CDS carburettor.
GEARBOX: Four-speed, floor-mounted gear change, automatic optional (with 1725 engine), synchromesh on all forward gears. Ratios, top 3.89:1, 3rd 5.41:1, 2nd 8.32:1, 1st 13.04:1, reverse 13.88:1.
REAR AXLE: Semi-floating, hypoid bevel, ratio saloon 3.89:1.

Instrument layout.

BRAKES: Lockheed, front 9.6in discs, rear 9in drums.
TYRES: 5.60 x 13.
SUSPENSION: Front fully independent coil spring and strut with integral telescopic shock absorbers, rear semi-elliptic leaf springs and telescopic shock absorbers.
STEERING: Burman recirculating ball.
DIMENSIONS: Length: 14ft (4267mm); **width:** 5ft 3.5in (1613mm); **height:** 4ft 8in (1422mm);

weight: saloon 18cwt 1qtr 4lb (929kg, dry 888kg), estate 19cwt 2qtr 9lb (995kg, dry 954kg); **turning circle:** 36ft (11m).
CAPACITIES: Fuel 10 gallons (45 litres). Boot: saloon 18ft³ (0.6m³), estate 34 or 62ft³ (0.94 or 1.7m³).

Floor gear change layout.

Hillman Husky (1954-1957)

The original Husky introduced in 1954 was effectively a shortened version of the mark 8 Hillman Minx estate.

ENGINE/GEARBOX: Four-cylinder, SV, bore 65mm, stroke 95mm, 1265cc, maximum bhp 35 at 4100rpm. Four-speed, floor-mounted gear change, synchromesh on top three gears. Ratios: top 4.78:1, 3rd 7.13:1, 2nd 11.81:1, 1st 17.05:1, reverse 22.73:1.
BRAKES: Lockheed, front and rear 8in drums.
TYRES: 5.00 x 15.
STEERING: Worm and Peg.
DIMENSIONS: Length: 12ft 3.5in (3747mm); **width:** 5ft 3.5in (1613mm); **height:** 4ft 8in (1422mm).

Instruments shown here include optional ammeter.

Floor gear change layout.

Hillman Husky series 1 (1959)

Introduced in 1958, and based on the new series Minx, it had the OHV engine introduced with the mark 8 Minx saloon, but, unlike the series Minx, the Husky would retain the engine as a 1390cc unit for series 2 and 3 models. Optional extras: heater, radio, clock, sliding rear quarter lights, overriders, exterior driving mirror, starting handle, white-wall tyres, rim finishers, and more.

COLOURS (1959): Two-tones: Caramel/Regency beige, and following with Foam white centre

section, Apple green, Powder blue, Charcoal, Ember red. Single tones: Caramel, Apple green, Powder blue, Ember red, Foam white.

ENGINE: Four-cylinder, OHV, bore 76.2mm, stroke 76.2mm, 1390cc, maximum bhp 43.5 at 4200rpm, Zenith 30VMG downdraught carburettor (later cars 51bhp at 4400rpm, Zenith 30VIG).
GEARBOX: Four-speed, floor-mounted gear change, synchromesh on top three gears. Ratios: top 4.55:1, 3rd 6.905:1, 2nd 10.618:1, 1st 16.599:1, reverse 21.026:1.
REAR AXLE: Semi-floating, spiral bevel, ratio 4.55:1 (series 1 and early series 2).
BRAKES: Lockheed, front and rear 8in drums.
TYRES: 5.60 x 15.
SUSPENSION: Front coil springs, swinging links and telescopic shock absorbers, rear semi-elliptic leaf springs with Armstrong lever arm shock absorbers.
STEERING: Burman recirculating ball.
DIMENSIONS: Length: 12ft 5.5in (3797mm); **width:** 5ft 1in (1549mm); **height:** 5ft 2in (1575mm); **weight:** 18cwt 2qtr 8lb (943kg); **turning circle:** 33ft 6in (10.2m).
CAPACITIES: Fuel 6.25 gallons (28 litres). Boot 19ft^3 (0.6m^3) or 41.5ft^3 (1.2m^3) with rear seat folded down.

Hillman Husky series 2

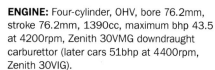

The series 2 was introduced in 1960, and replaced by the face-lifted, but technically similar, series 3 in 1963. Compared to the series 1, this car featured a larger rear window and windscreen, a slightly lowered roof line with ribbed rear roof, headlamp hoods, a different front grille, and better seats. It was also 15lb heavier. Optional extras: heater/ventilation equipment, radio, clock, sliding rear quarter lights, overriders, starting handle, whitewall tyres, and more.

COLOURS (1961): All with Foam white centre section, Glen green, Lake blue, Powder blue, Venetian red, Charcoal.
Note: later series 2 cars had Azure blue instead of Lake blue.

1962 specification
ENGINE: Four-cylinder, OHV, bore 76.2mm, stroke 76.2mm, 1390cc, maximum bhp 43.5 at 4200rpm Zenith 26 VME downdraught carburettor (pre 1962 cars 51bhp at 4400rpm, Zenith 30VIG).

Note: three different Zenith carburettors were used during the life of the series 1 and 2 models.
GEARBOX: Four-speed, floor-mounted gear change, synchromesh on top three gears. Ratios: top 4.22:1, 3rd 5.88:1, 2nd 9.04:1, 1st 15.82:1, reverse 21.09:1; early cars: top 4.55, 3rd 6.34, 2nd 9.75, 1st 15.24, reverse 19.31.
REAR AXLE: Semi-floating, hypoid bevel ratio 4.22:1, early 1960 cars, spiral bevel, ratio 4.55:1.
BRAKES: Lockheed, front and rear 8in drums.
TYRES: 5.60 x 15.
SUSPENSION: Front coil springs, swinging links and telescopic shock absorbers, rear semi-elliptic leaf springs with Armstrong lever arm shock absorbers.
STEERING: Burman recirculating ball.
DIMENSIONS: Length: 12ft 5.5in (3797mm); **width:** 5ft 1in (1549mm); **height:** 4ft 11.5in (1511mm); **weight:** 18cwt 2qtr 8lb (943kg); **turning circle:** 33ft 6in (10.2m).

Floor gear change layout.

Instrument layout (right) includes optional temperature gauge.

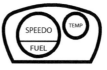

Hillman Husky series 3

Introduced in 1963 and discontinued in 1965, the series 3 featured revised facia and instrumentation, the restyled front end from the series 5 Minx, improved suspension and elimination of greasing points, but it retained the series 2 drum brakes all round. It had 15in wheels, although the Minx had changed to 13in, and the 1390cc engine introduced with the series 1, albeit with a different Zenith carburettor developing 43.5bhp at 4200rpm.

COLOURS (1963): Two-tones all with Foam white centre section, Glen green, Forest green, Azure blue, Pippin red, Charcoal. Single tone, Foam white.
ENGINE: Four-cylinder, OHV, bore 76.2mm, stroke 76.2mm, 1390cc, maximum bhp 43.5 at 4200rpm Zenith 30VNN downdraught carburettor.
GEARBOX: Four-speed, floor-mounted gear

change, (all synchromesh from late 1964). Ratios: top 4.22:1, 3rd 5.88:1, 2nd 9.04:1, 1st 15.82:1, reverse 21.09:1.
REAR AXLE: Semi-floating, hypoid bevel ratio 4.22:1.
BRAKES: Lockheed, front and rear 8in drums.
TYRES: 5.60 x 15.
SUSPENSION: Front coil springs, wishbones and Woodhead-Monroe telescopic shock absorbers, rear semi-elliptic leaf springs with Armstrong lever arm shock absorbers.
STEERING: Burman recirculating ball.
DIMENSIONS: Length: 12ft 5.5in (3797mm); **width:** 5ft 1in (1549mm); **height:** 4ft 11.5in (1511mm); **weight:** 18cwt 2qtr 8lb (943kg); **turning circle:** 33ft 6in (10.2m).
CAPACITIES: Fuel 6.25 gallons (28 litres). Boot 18ft³ (0.6m³) or 40ft³ (1.2m³) with rear seat folded down.

Instrument layout.

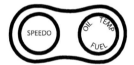

Hillman Super Minx mark 1

Introduced in 1961, this car was originally intended to replace the Minx, but instead the decision was taken to continue with the Minx and introduce the Super Minx saloon as a separate model. An estate and convertible were added in 1962, shortly before the introduction of the mark 2. Unlike the Minx, the spare wheel was now in a cradle under the boot, exposed to mud thrown up from the road, but, on a positive note, it meant you did not end up putting a wet wheel in the boot if you got a puncture and needed to change wheels when it was raining! Optional extras: heater, radio, clock, oil pressure gauge, ammeter, headlamp flasher, column gear change, Smiths Easidrive automatic transmission, reversing light, overriders, whitewall tyres, wheel trim discs, and more.

29

COLOURS (1961): Saloon: two-tone, lower body colour first, Glen green/Foam white, Azure blue/Foam white, Morocco brown/ Regency beige, Foam white/Azure blue. Single tones, Embassy black, Powder blue, Foam white, Azure blue, Glen green, Thistle grey.

ENGINE: Four-cylinder, OHV, bore 81.5mm, stroke 76.2mm, 1592cc, maximum bhp 66.25 at 4800rpm, Zenith 32VN downdraught carburettor.

Above: A cylindrical boot lock identifies a mark 1 externally.

GEARBOX: Four-speed, floor-mounted gear change (steering column change optional), synchromesh on top three gears. Ratios: top 4.22:1, 3rd 5.88:1, 2nd 9.04:1, 1st 14.13:1, reverse 17.896:1.

REAR AXLE: Semi-floating, hypoid bevel, ratio 4.22:1.
BRAKES: Lockheed 9in front and rear drums.
TYRES: 5.90 x 13.
SUSPENSION: Front coil springs and swinging links, rear semi-elliptic leaf springs, telescopic shock absorbers all round.

STEERING: Burman recirculating ball.
DIMENSIONS: Length: 13ft 9in (4191mm); **width:** 5ft 2.25in (1581mm); **height:** 4ft 10.25in (1479mm); **weight:** 1 ton 1cwt 1qtr 20lb (1087kg); **turning circle:** 36ft (10.97m).
CAPACITIES: Fuel 11 gallons (50 litres). Boot 14.5ft³ (0.41m³).

See Super Minx mark 2 for dashboard diagram.

Left: Floor gear change layout (standard). Right: Steering column automatic gear change layout, (optional).

Hillman Super Minx mark 2

The Super Minx mark 2 was introduced in 1962 to replace the mark 1. Improvements included front disc brakes, elimination of all greasing points, individual front seats, headlamp flasher, and, by repositioning the fuel tank, the luggage space was increased. Borg-Warner automatic transmission replaced

The Super Minx mark 1 and 2 (left) and the Super Minx mark 3 and 4 (right). Note: not only the flatter roof line and more vertical, larger windscreen on the later cars, but also the difference in the top half of the doors, and inclusion of rear quarter lights in the rear door in the earlier models.

the Smiths Easidrive. The handbrake remained by the right-hand side of the driver's seat,

and steering column gear change was optional, but without the bench seat of the mark 1 there was no way of squeezing three people in the front. It was replaced by the squarer-styled mark 3 in 1964. Standard equipment included a heater with two-speed fan (fitted as standard following introduction of mark 1 estate and convertible models), screen washers, headlamp flasher, individual front seats, childproof door locks, two padded sun visors, disc brakes. Optional extras: radio, clock, oil pressure gauge, ammeter, seat belts, Borg-Warner automatic transmission, reversing light, overriders, whitewall tyres, wheel trim discs, and more.

COLOURS (1962): Convertible: Fiesta blue/blue hood, Pippin red/red or black hood, Seacrest green/green hood, Summer yellow/black hood, Moonstone/blue, red or black hood.

COLOURS (1963): Saloon: (early 1963 only †, late 1963 only *) two-tone, lower body colour first, Glen green/Foam white, Azure blue/Foam white, Morocco brown/Regency beige, Foam white/Azure blue, Fiesta blue/Foam white†, Pippin red/Birch grey†, Pippin red/Foam white*, Birch grey/Pippin red*, Sage green/Forest green*. Single tones, Embassy black, Azure blue, Foam white, Fiesta blue†, Glen green†, Birch grey†, Forest green*, Thistle grey*. Estate: two-tone, main body colour first, Azure blue/Foam white, Glen green/Foam white, Pippin red/Foam white, Thistle grey/Foam white†, Sage green/Foam white*, Birch grey/Charcoal*. Single tones, Glen green, Azure blue, Thistle grey†, Foam white*, Forest green*, Birch grey*.

Instrument layout. Some gauges are optional equipment.

ENGINE: Four-cylinder, OHV, bore 81.5mm, stroke 76.2mm, 1592cc, maximum bhp 62 at 4400rpm, Solex 33PSEI downdraught carburettor.
GEARBOX: Four-speed, floor-mounted gear change (steering column change optional), synchromesh on top three gears. Ratios: top 3.89:1, 3rd 5.41:1, 2nd 8.32:1, 1st 13.01:1, reverse 16.483:1; estate & later saloon/convertible: top 4.22, 3rd 5.88, 2nd 4.04, 1st 14.13, reverse 17.89.
REAR AXLE: Semi-floating, hypoid bevel, ratio 3.89:1; estate & later saloon/convertible 4.22:1.
BRAKES: Lockheed, front 10.3in discs, rear 9in drums.
TYRES: saloon 6.00 x 13, estate 6.50 x 13.
SUSPENSION: Front coil springs and swinging links, rear semi-elliptic leaf springs, telescopic shock absorbers all round.
STEERING: Burman recirculating ball.
DIMENSIONS: Length: 13ft 9in (4191mm); **width:** 5ft 2.25in (1581mm); **height:** saloon/estate 4ft 10.25in (1479mm); **height:** convertible 4ft 9.25in (1454mm); **weight:** saloon 1 ton 1cwt 0qtr 5lb (1067kg, dry 1026kg), convertible 1 ton 1cwt 2qtr 20lb (1101kg, dry 1058kg); **turning circle:** 36ft (10.97m).
CAPACITIES: Fuel 10.5 gallons (48 litres), estate 10 gallons (45 litres). Boot: saloon/convertible 16ft³ (0.45m³), estate 28.5 or 46ft³ with rear seat folded down (0.8 or 1.4m³).

Left: floor gear change layout (standard). Right: steering column gear change layout (optional).

Hillman Super Minx mark 3

The Super Minx mark 3 was introduced in 1964, to replace the mark 2. The convertible was deleted from the range, changes from the mark 2 included a squarer look, the result of changes to the front and rear glass area, a new two-tone paint scheme, an all-synchromesh gearbox, and reclining front seats. Standard equipment included a heater with two-speed fan, screen washers, headlamp flasher, fully reclining front seats, overriders, and wheel trims. Optional extras: radio, clock, oil pressure gauge, ammeter, seat belts, Laycock overdrive, Borg-Warner automatic transmission, reversing lights, whitewall tyres, and more.

COLOURS (1964): Saloon/estate: two-tone, main body colour first, Azure blue/Artic white, Forest green/Sage green, Sage green/Forest green, Storm grey/Alabaster grey, Alabaster grey/Forest green, Tartan red/Embassy black. Single tones, Artic white, Forest green, Azure blue, Alabaster grey, Tartan red. Saloon only: two-tone, main body colour first, Kingfisher blue/Embassy black, Slate blue/Dawn mist, Artic white/Tartan red. Single tones, Embassy black, Storm grey, Slate blue, Kingfisher blue, Sage green.

ENGINE: Four-cylinder, OHV, bore 81.5mm, stroke 76.2mm, 1592cc, maximum bhp 62 at 4400rpm, Solex 33PSEI downdraught carburettor.

GEARBOX: Four-speed, floor-mounted gear change, overdrive or automatic optional, synchromesh on all forward gears. Ratios: top 4.22:1, 3rd 5.88:1, 2nd 9.04:1, 1st 14.15:1, reverse 15.07:1.

REAR AXLE: Semi-floating, hypoid bevel, ratio 4.22:1.

BRAKES: Lockheed, front 10.3in discs, rear 9in drums.

TYRES: saloon 6.00 x 13, estate 6.50 x 13.

SUSPENSION: Front coil springs and swinging links, rear semi-elliptic leaf springs, telescopic shock absorbers all round.

STEERING: Burman recirculating ball.

DIMENSIONS: Length: 13ft 10.25in (4223mm); width: 5ft 2.25in (1581mm); height: 4ft 10in (1473mm); weight: saloon 1 ton 0cwt 3qtr 24lb (1065kg, dry 1021kg), estate 1 ton 1cwt 3qtr 18lb (1113kg, dry 1072kg); **turning circle:** 36ft (10.97m). **CAPACITIES:** Fuel 10.5 gallons (48 litres), estate 10 gallons (45 litres). Boot saloon 16ft³ (0.45m³), estate 28.5 or 46ft³ with rear seat folded down (0.8 or 1.4m³).

Above, steering column automatic gear change layout, (optional). Standard floor gear change as mark 4.

Hillman Super Minx mark 4

Introduced in 1965, the mark 4 replaced the Super Minx mark 3 to which it was visually identical, it now had a larger engine of 1725cc with a five bearing crankshaft instead of three. The saloon was discontinued in 1966 following the introduction of the Hillman Hunter, the estate continued until 1967 when the new Minx estate was launched. Standard equipment included heater with two-speed fan, screen washers, headlamp flasher, fully reclining front seats, overriders, and wheel trims. Optional extras: radio, clock, oil pressure gauge, ammeter, seat belts, overdrive, automatic transmission, reversing lights, whitewall tyres, and more.

COLOURS (1965): Saloon/estate: two-tone, main body colour first, Bermuda blue/Artic white, Storm grey/Alabaster grey, Willow green/ Forest green, Forest green/Willow green, Tartan red/Embassy black. Single tones, Artic white, Alabaster grey, Forest green, Tartan red. **COLOURS (1966):** Estate: Single tone only, Willow green, Bermuda blue, Shore beige, Tartan red, Polar white. **ENGINE:** Four-cylinder, OHV, bore 81.5mm, stroke 82.5mm, 1725cc, maximum bhp 69.5 at 4800rpm, Zenith downdraught carburettor.

GEARBOX: Four-speed, floor-mounted gear change, overdrive or automatic optional, synchromesh on all forward gears. Ratios: top 4.22:1, 3rd 5.88:1, 2nd 9.04:1, 1st 14.15:1, reverse 15.07:1. **REAR AXLE:** Semi-floating, hypoid bevel, ratio 4.22:1. **BRAKES:** Lockheed, front 10.3in discs, rear 9in drums. **TYRES:** saloon 6.00 x 13, estate 6.50 x 13. **SUSPENSION:** Front coil springs and swinging links, rear-semi-elliptic leaf springs, telescopic shock absorbers all round.

STEERING: Burman recirculating ball.
DIMENSIONS: Length: 13ft 10.25in
(4223mm); **width:** 5ft 2.25in (1581mm);
height: 4ft 10in (1473mm); **weight:** estate 1
ton 1cwt 3qtr 27lb (1117kg); **turning circle:**
36ft (10.97m).
CAPACITIES: Fuel 10.5 gallons (48 litres).
Boot saloon 16ft³ (0.45m³), estate 28.5
or 46ft³ with rear seat folded down (0.8 or
1.4m³).

Floor gear change layout.

Instrument layout.

Note: handbrake by the side of driver's seat is a typical Rootes feature in the 1960s.

The name 'Paykan' is also sometimes spelled Peykan or Paykann.

Paykan

The Hunter was assembled in Iran as the
Paykan from 1967 until April 2005! Initially
available as a Deluxe or Standard model
by 1971 the range had extended to Deluxe,
Standard, GT, Taxi and Pick-up, an automatic
model was also available from 1970. The
vehicle shown here is a typical early model.
Later models featured large plastic bumpers
like those used on the Morris Ital when it
replaced the Marina. The Paykan originally
used a Hunter 1725 engine with 62bhp, this
was followed by a version of the 1796cc
engine used in the Peugeot 504 and then
the Avenger 1598 engine with 65bhp was
adopted. Overleaf the many changing faces
of the Hunter from introduction in 1966 to
end of production in 1979.

Outside the original Archive Centre Trust building near Banbury – a replica of the Hunter that won the 1968 London to Sydney Rally.

The many changing faces of the Hunter from introduction in 1966 to end of production in 1979.

Hunter mark 1 1966-1967.

Hunter 1967-1971.

Hunter (non GLS) 1972-1973.

Hunter GLS 1972-1973.

Hunter 1974-1977.

Chrysler Hunter 1977-1979.

Hillman Hunter mark 1

Introduced in 1966 to replace the Super Minx, the Hunter mark 1 had a short life of just one year, much like that of many Rootes vehicles that had preceded it, and unlike that of the mark 2 which followed it in 1967. Like the Super Minx the jacking points remained under the bumpers, much safer than standing at the side of the car if you needed to change a wheel and not likely to sink into soft ground at the side of the road either, but the spare wheel was now in the boot instead of underneath it. The Hunter and Vogue were the first of the 'Arrow' range of cars to be launched with Humber and Sunbeam variants appearing in 1967 it was also the first Rootes car to feature MacPherson strut front suspension a system that was not adopted by BMC or Vauxhall for another ten years but which Ford had been using since 1950. Note that the only model available was a saloon; and the Hunter name was originally used by Singer, on a car in production when the company was acquired by Rootes. Standard equipment included heater, fresh-air ventilation system

The red Hunter above has been fitted with a non-standard vinyl roof covering, a sunroof, alloy wheels, etc.

with swivelling vents in dashboard, two-speed wipers, and fully reclining front seats. Optional extras: radio, oil pressure gauge, ammeter, seat belts, Laycock overdrive, Borg-Warner automatic transmission, reversing lights, mud flaps, and more.

COLOURS (1966): Embassy black, Storm grey, Willow green, Tartan red, Polar white, Bermuda blue, Shore beige, Neptune green, Oxford blue.

ENGINE: Four-cylinder, OHV, bore 81.5mm, stroke 82.5mm, 1725cc, maximum bhp 80 at 5000rpm, Stromberg 150CDS carburettor.

GEARBOX: Four-speed, floor-mounted gear change, overdrive or automatic transmission optional, synchromesh on all forward gears. Ratios: top 3.7:1, 3rd 5.14:1, 2nd 7.92:1, 1st 12.4:1, reverse 13.21:1.

REAR AXLE: Semi-floating, hypoid bevel, ratio 3.7:1.

BRAKES: Lockheed, front 9.6in discs, rear 9in drums.

TYRES: 5.60 x 13.

SUSPENSION: Front MacPherson strut, coil springs and telescopic dampers with anti-roll bar, rear semi-elliptic leaf springs with telescopic shock absorbers.

STEERING: Burman recirculating ball.

DIMENSIONS: Length: 14ft 1in (4292mm); **width:** 5ft 3.5in (1613mm); **height:** 4ft 8in (1422mm); **weight:** 18cwt 1qtr 16lb (934kg); turning circle: 32.5ft (10.2m).

CAPACITIES: Fuel 10 gallons (45 litres). Boot 18ft^3 (0.5m^3).

Instrument layout (including optional gauges).

A Hillman Hunter mark 2 (technical details as mark 1, but with power-assisted brakes from 1968).

Hillman Hunter (1970)

Introduced in 1970 to replace the Hunter mark 2 to which it appeared identical, this Hunter was expanded into a range with different specifications to replace the discontinued Minx, Gazelle and Vogue. The range consisted of the Deluxe with 1500 engine, Super and GL with 1725 engine, GT with twin carburettor 1725 engine, and Deluxe and GL estates. The Hunter name had originally been a Singer name in the 1950s, so perhaps it is appropriate that the Vogue was renamed as a Hunter. Standard equipment (1970 Deluxe) heater, fresh-air ventilation system with swivelling vents in dashboard, screen washer, headlamp flasher, steering column lock, rear door childproof locks, and more.

Super adds: centre console, two-speed wipers, two-speed blower, wood covered fascia. GL, in addition to Super: lockable glovebox with light, twin horns, reclining front seats, opening quarter lights, reversing lights, wheel trim discs. Optional extras, all models: heated rear screen, automatic transmission, metallic paint, and more. GL and GT only: overdrive.

COLOURS (1971-1972): Polar white, Embassy black, Tahiti blue, Baltic blue, Carib blue, Oasis green, Limelight, Golden olive, Safari beige, Firecracker, Sundance, Sunset, and metallics Silver grey, Pewter, Electric blue, Aquarios,

In 1970 the Hillman Minx became the Hunter Deluxe, the original Hillman Hunter became the Super, and the GL replaced the Singer Vogue. There was no replacement for the discontinued Singer Gazelle. The GT and GLS were new additional models.

Instrument layout for GL model.

Opposite page, all GL models; this page, above, is a GT model. All below are Deluxe estates. Note: Deluxe models had non-opening front quarter lights.

Floor gear change layouts, manual on left and optional automatic on right.

Cedar green, Aztec gold, Tangerine, Phantom mist, Spice.
Note: some colours were only available on specific models, eg GL.
ENGINE: All four-cylinder, OHV. Deluxe: bore 81.5mm, stroke 71.6mm, 1496cc, maximum bhp 64 at 4800rpm, Stromberg 150CDS carburettor. Super: cast iron cylinder head, bore 81.5mm, stroke 82.5mm, 1725cc, maximum bhp 71 at 4900rpm, Stromberg 150CDS carburettor. GL: aluminium cylinder head, bore 81.5mm, stroke 82.5mm, 1725cc, maximum bhp 77 at 5000rpm, Stromberg 150CDS carburettor. GT: as GL except maximum bhp 94 at 5200rpm, twin Stromberg 150CDS carburettors.
GEARBOX: Four-speed, floor-mounted gear change, overdrive or automatic transmission optional, synchromesh on all forward gears. Ratios: GL saloon & GT, top 3.7:1, 3rd 5.15:1, 2nd 7.92:1, 1st 12.41:1, reverse 13.2:1. GL saloon and Estate with overdrive, o/d, top 3.12:1, top 3.89:1, o/d 3rd 4.38:1, 3rd 5.41:1, 2nd 8.32:1, 1st 13.04:1, reverse 13.88:1. DL and Super saloons & GL estate, top 3.89:1, 3rd 5.41:1, 2nd 8.32:1, 1st 13.04:1, reverse 13.88:1; DL estate, top 4.22:1, 3rd 5.87:1, 2nd 9.03:1, 1st 14.15:1, reverse 15.06:1.
REAR AXLE: Semi-floating, hypoid bevel, ratios: GL saloon and GT 3.7:1, with overdrive 3.89:1, Deluxe and Super saloons and GL estate, 3.89:1, Deluxe estate 4.22:1, all automatic models 3.89:1 except GL saloon 3.7:1.
BRAKES: Lockheed, front 9.6in discs, rear 9in drums (servo assisted).
TYRES: Saloons 5.60 x 13, estates 6.00 x 13, GT 165 x 13.
SUSPENSION: Front MacPherson strut, coil springs and telescopic dampers with anti-roll bar, rear semi-elliptic leaf springs with telescopic shock absorbers.
STEERING: Burman recirculating ball.
DIMENSIONS: Length: saloon without overriders 14ft 0in (4267mm), estate 14ft 2.75in (4337mm); **width:** 5ft 3.5in (1613mm); **height:** 4ft 8in (1422mm); **weight:** according to model, Deluxe saloon 18cwt 26lb (926kg), GL estate 19 cwt 2 qtr 14 lb (997kg); **turning circle:** 34ft (10.36m).
CAPACITIES: Fuel 10 gallons (45 litres). Boot 18ft^3 (0.5m^3).

Hillman Hunter (1972)

New in 1972 was a revised grille featuring two rectangular sections, and a new model, the GLS, fitted with the Rapier H120 engine. It was easily identified by its twin headlamps and Sceptre-like grille at the front, and a black panel at the rear. Its Rostyle wheels can be found on many cars of this era. For 1974 a four-speed replaced the three-speed automatic option. Standard equipment (1972 in addition to Deluxe model): Super: centre console, two-speed wipers, two-speed blower, side mouldings. GL and GLS: centre console, wood veneer trim, two-speed wipers, two-speed blower, lockable glovebox, twin horns, fully reclining front seats, cigarette lighter, interior bonnet release, reversing lights, wheel trim discs, side mouldings. GT: centre console, two-speed wipers, two-speed blower, twin horns, body side stripes. Instruments: Deluxe and Super, speedometer, fuel and water temperature gauges. GL, speedometer with mileage trip recorder, ammeter, fuel and water temperature gauges. GLS and GT, speedometer with mileage trip recorder, revolution counter, ammeter, fuel, water and oil pressure gauges. Optional extras all models, radio, seat belts, heated rear window, vinyl roof.

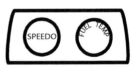

This page GL model, opposite page Deluxe & GLS models.

COLOURS (1973): Included Honey gold, Platinum, Carib blue, Grasshopper green.
ENGINE: All four-cylinder, OHV. Deluxe: bore 81.5mm, stroke 71.6mm, 1496cc, maximum bhp 64 at 4800rpm, Stromberg 150CDS carburettor. Super: cast iron cylinder head, bore 81.5mm, stroke 82.5mm, 1725cc, maximum bhp 71 at 4900rpm, Stromberg 150CDS carburettor. GL: aluminium cylinder head, bore 81.5mm, stroke 82.5mm, 1725cc, maximum bhp 82 at 5300rpm, Stromberg 150D3 carburettor. GT: as GL except maximum bhp 92 at 5400rpm, twin Stromberg 150CD3 carburettors. GLS: as GL except maximum bhp 108 at 5200rpm, twin Weber 40DCOE carburettors, four branch exhaust manifold.
GEARBOX: Four-speed, floor-mounted gear change, overdrive or automatic transmission optional, synchromesh on all forward gears. Ratios: GL saloon, top 3.7:1, 3rd 5.15:1, 2nd

Instrument layout for DL & Super.

Instrument layout for GT & GLS.

Rostyle wheel for GLS model, but owners often change the wheels, so lesser models can be found with these fitted.

Above, a Deluxe model; below are GLS.

7.92:1, 1st 12.41:1, reverse 13.2:1; GLS and GT, top 3.7:1, 3rd 4.79:1, 2nd 7.37:1, 1st 11.55:1, reverse 12.29:1; DL and Super saloons, GL estate, top 3.89:1, 3rd 5.41:1, 2nd 8.32:1, 1st 13.04:1, reverse 13.88:1; DL estate, top 4.22:1, 3rd 5.87:1, 2nd 9.03:1, 1st 14.15:1, reverse 15.07:1; with overdrive: GL saloon and Estate, GLS & GT as 1974 models.

REAR AXLE: Semi-floating, hypoid bevel, ratios: GL saloon, GLS and GT, 3.7:1; DL & Super saloons, GL estate, 3.89:1; DL estate 4.22:1.

BRAKES: Lockheed, power assisted (except Deluxe and Super saloons), front 9.6in discs, rear 9in drums.

TYRES: DL, Super and GL saloons, 5.60 x 13; DL and GL estates, 6.00 x 13, GT 155 x 13, GLS 165 x 13.

SUSPENSION: Front MacPherson strut, coil springs and telescopic dampers with anti-roll bar, rear semi-elliptic leaf springs with telescopic shock absorbers.

STEERING: Burman recirculating ball.

DIMENSIONS: Length: saloon without over-riders 14ft 0in (4267mm), estate 14ft 2.75in (4337mm); **width:** 5ft 3.5in (1613mm); **height:** 4ft 8in (1422mm); **weight:** according to model 18cwt 19lb to 19cwt 2qtr 17lb (923 to 998kg); **turning circle:** 34ft (10.36m).

CAPACITIES: Fuel 10 gallons (45 litres). Boot saloon 18ft^3 (0.5m^3), estate 34 or 62ft^3 (0.94 or 1.7m^3).

Hillman Hunter (1974)

The 1974 version entailed yet another styling change: another front grille and changes to the rear panel, together with new bumpers. A heated rear window was now standard, and there were equipment upgrades all round, all models now had an interior bonnet release. It was replaced in 1977 by the Chrysler Hunter, available only as DL and Super saloons, with similar frontal treatment to the earlier GLS models, and was eventually discontinued in 1979. Standard equipment (1974) all models, heater with two-speed blower (single-speed on Deluxe), two-speed wipers, electric screen washers, headlamp flasher, hazard flashers, heated rear window. Super adds, centre console. GL adds, trip recorder, ammeter, centre console, lockable glovebox with light, cigar lighter, dipping mirror, reclining front seats, cloth seat inserts, opening front door quarter lights, reversing light. GT adds: trip recorder, oil pressure gauge, rev counter, ammeter, centre console, dipping mirror, reversing light. GLS in addition to GT: lockable glovebox with light, cigar lighter, reclining front seats, cloth seat inserts, opening front door quarter lights. Optional extras: radio, Borg-Warner automatic transmission, fog lamps, vinyl roof, and more.

COLOURS (1975): Polar white, Lavender, Carib blue, Imperial red, Cherry, Magenta, Apricot, Orange blossom, Sunflower, and metallics – Copperbeech, Champagne, Peppermint, Pinewood, Kingfisher.
ENGINE: All four-cylinder, OHV. Deluxe: bore

81.5mm, stroke 71.6mm, 1496cc, maximum bhp 64 at 4800rpm, Stromberg 150CD3 or SU HS4/C carburettor. Super: cast iron cylinder head, bore 81.5mm, stroke 82.5mm, 1725cc, maximum bhp 71 at 4900rpm, Stromberg 150CD3 carburettor. GL (and Super from 1975): aluminium cylinder head, bore 81.5mm, stroke 82.5mm, capacity 1725cc, maximum bhp 82 at 5300rpm, Stromberg 150CD3 or SU HS4 carburettor. GT:

The Copperbeech car is a Topaz special edition model with vinyl roof covering, sports wheels, side repeater indicators, radio and overdrive as standard equipment.

Instrument layout for GLS.

Instrument layout for Super models.

The Estate model has a Humber Sceptre style tailgate with mock wood trim, but wears Chrysler GL badges.

as GL except maximum bhp 92 at 5400rpm, twin Stromberg 150CD3 carburettors. GLS: as GL except maximum bhp 108 at 5200rpm, twin Weber 40DCOE carburettors, four branch exhaust manifold.

GEARBOX: Four-speed, floor-mounted gear change, overdrive or automatic transmission optional, synchromesh on all forward gears. Ratios: GL saloon, top 3.7:1, 3rd 5.15, 2nd 7.92, 1st 12.41, reverse 13.2; with overdrive, o/d, top 3.10, top 3.89, o/d 3rd 4.31, 3rd 5.41, 2nd 8.33, 1st 13.04, reverse 13.88. GLS and GT, top 3.7:1, 3rd 4.79, 2nd 7.37, 1st 11.55, reverse 12.29. GLS with overdrive, o/d, top 3.10, top 3.89, o/d 3rd 4.02, 3rd 5.04, 2nd 7.75, 1st 12.14, reverse 12.92; GT with overdrive, o/d, top 3.36, top 4.22, o/d 3rd 4.36, 3rd 5.47, 2nd 8.41, 1st 13.18, reverse 14.03; DL and Super saloons, GL estate, top 3.89:1, 3rd 5.41, 2nd 8.32, 1st 13.04, reverse 13.88; DL estate, top 4.22, 3rd 5.87, 2nd 9.04, 1st 14.15, reverse 15.06.

REAR AXLE: Semi-floating, hypoid bevel, ratios: GL saloon, GLS and GT, 3.7:1; DL & Super saloons, GL estate, 3.89:1; DL estate, 4.22:1; models with overdrive GL, GLS, 3.89:1, GT, 4.22:1; all automatic transmissions, same rear axle ratios as manual models.

BRAKES: Lockheed, power assisted (except DL and Super saloon), front 9.6in discs, rear 9in drums.

TYRES: DL, Super, GL and GT saloons 155 x 13, DL and GL estates and GLS 165 x 13.

SUSPENSION: Front MacPherson strut, coil springs and telescopic dampers with anti-roll bar, rear semi-elliptic leaf springs with telescopic shock absorbers.

STEERING: Burman recirculating ball.

DIMENSIONS: Length: saloon 14ft 3in (4343mm), estate 14ft 5in (4394mm); **width:** 5ft 3.5in (1613mm); **height:** 4ft 8in (1422mm); **weight:** according to model 18cwt 0lb to 19cwt 2qtr 7lb (914 to 994kg); **turning circle:** 34ft (10.36m).

CAPACITIES: Fuel 10 gallons (45 litres). Boot saloon 18ft^3 (0.5m^3), estate 34 or 62ft^3 with rear seat folded down (0.94 or 1.7m^3).

Floor gear change layout.

Hillman Imp

Introduced in 1963 as Rootes' answer to the Mini (and other small cars of the period), in true 1960's form there had to be badge-engineered versions of the basic car: enter the Singer Chamois and Sunbeam Imp Sport. In 1965, the Rally Imp, Super Imp and mark 2 Deluxe were introduced. In 1968 changes were made to the interior, Super models received a new front and rear trim. The Imp was discontinued in 1976. Reliability problems with the engine are legendary and with hindsight rear engined, rear-wheel drive was probably not the way to go, but let us not forget that it had a certain amount of racing success and was a very practical car with opening rear window, folding rear seat and storage pockets in the doors, the latter made possible by moving the handbrake from the right side of the driver's seat, where it had been in previous Hillmans, to the space between the front seats. Imp Deluxe standard equipment at launch included a heater, screen washers, two sun visors, and four stowage pockets. Optional extras: radio, seat belts, reversing light, overriders, whitewall tyres, wheel trims (standard on Super Imp), and more.

The engine was designed by Coventry Climax, manufacturers of auxiliary fire-pump engines, who went on to develop engines for Lotus and Formula 1.

Above: Imp mark 1.

Instrument layout, early cars.

As introduced from 1965, below, Imp mark 2; bottom, Super Imp. Imp models from Oct 1968, onwards are featured on opposite page, top two are Super Imp and lower two are Deluxe models.

Although the Deluxe retained its original equipment when the Super Imp was launched in 1965, a 1969 brochure lists the Deluxe as having only two stowage pockets and rubber mat flooring with the Super model having gained a lockable glovebox and retaining its four stowage pockets and carpets. During 1974 a heated rear window was fitted across the entire range, while in 1975 the Deluxe got its carpets back and the Super received reversing lights.

COLOURS (1963): Foam white, Embassy black, Glenalmond green, Tartan red, Loch blue, Skye blue, Balmoral grey (fair enough, it was built in Scotland).

COLOURS (1965): Super Imp: Polar white, Forest green, Orchid green, Loch blue, Capri blue, Maroon, Embassy black. All Super models had a chrome side flash with Black insert.

ENGINE: (All models except Rally Imp) Four-cylinder, OHC (rear-mounted), bore 68mm, stroke 60.4mm, 875cc, maximum bhp 42 at 5000rpm, Solex B30PIHT (autochoke) or Solex B30PIH5 downdraught carburettor.

GEARBOX/REAR AXLE: Four-speed, floor-mounted gear change, synchromesh on all forward gears, combined gearbox and hypoid bevel transaxle. Ratios: top 4.138:1, 3rd 5.702:1, 2nd 8.905:1, 1st 16.595:1, reverse 13.824:1, final drive 4.857:1.

ENGINE: (Rally Imp only): Four-cylinder, OHC, bore 72.5mm, stroke 60.4mm, 998cc, maximum bhp 65 at 6200rpm, Twin Stromberg 150 CD carburettors.

GEARBOX: (Four-speed) ratios: top 4.48:1, 3rd 6.19:1, 2nd 8.905:1, 1st 16.595:1, reverse 13.824:1.

BRAKES: Girling front and rear 8in drums.

TYRES: 5.50 x 12.

SUSPENSION: Front independent coil springs and swing axle, rear independent coil springs and trailing links, telescopic shock absorbers all round.

STEERING: Rack and pinion.

DIMENSIONS (1963/1965): Length: 11ft 7in (3530mm); **width:** 5ft 0.25in (1530mm); **height:** 4ft 6.5in (1384mm); **weight:** Deluxe mark 1, 13cwt 3qtr 0lb (699kg), Deluxe mark 2, 14cwt 1lb (711kg), Super, 14cwt 10lb (716kg); **turning circle:** 30ft 6in (9.3m).

CAPACITIES: Fuel 6 gallons (27 litres). Boot front 3.25ft³, rear 5ft³ or 16.5ft³ with rear seat lowered (combined 0.25 or 0.6m³).

COLOURS (1975): Included Polar white, Apricot, Orange blossom, Cherry, Magenta, Sunflower, Lavender, Imperial red, Carib blue.

Instrument layout, later models.

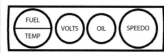

FUEL

TEMP

VOLTS

OIL

SPEEDO

Floor gear change layout.

Hillman Californian

Introduced in 1967 and discontinued in 1970, the Californian received a face-lift in 1968, along with interior revisions. Unlike the Imp the rear window was non opening, but it did have split folding rear seats. Standard equipment from the start included a heater, reclining front seats, four stowage pockets with armrests on rear pockets, and more.

ENGINE: Four-cylinder, OHC (rear-mounted), bore 68mm, stroke 60.35mm, 875cc, maximum bhp 42 at 5000rpm, Solex B30PIH5 downdraught carburettor.

GEARBOX/REAR AXLE: Four-speed, floor-mounted gear change, synchromesh on all forward gears, combined gearbox and hypoid bevel transaxle. Ratios: top 4.138:1, 3rd 5.702:1, 2nd 8.905:1, 1st 16.595:1, reverse 13.824:1, final drive 4.857:1.

BRAKES: Girling front and rear 8in drums.

TYRES: 5.50 x 12 tubeless.

SUSPENSION: Front independent coil springs and swing axle, rear independent coil springs and trailing links, telescopic shock absorbers all round.

STEERING: Rack and pinion.

DIMENSIONS (1969): Length: 11ft 7in (3530mm); **width:** 5ft 0.25in (1530mm); **height:** 4ft 4.5in (1334mm); **weight:** 14cwt 7lb (714kg); **turning circle:** 30ft 6in (9.3m).

CAPACITIES: Fuel 6 gallons (27 litres). Boot front 3.25ft³, rear 3.5ft³ or 15ft³ with rear seat lowered (combined 0.23 or 0.55m³).

Left and below: Later cars with revised front and rear trim.

Hillman Husky

Introduced in 1967 and discontinued in 1970, this was the estate version of the Imp.

ENGINE: Four-cylinder, OHC (rear-mounted), bore 68mm, stroke 60.35mm, 875cc, maximum bhp 42 at 5000rpm, Solex B30PIH5 downdraught carburettor.

GEARBOX/REAR AXLE: Four-speed, floor-mounted gear change, synchromesh on all forward gears, combined gearbox and hypoid bevel transaxle. Ratios: top 4.138:1, 3rd 5.702:1, 2nd 8.905:1, 1st 16.595:1, reverse 13.824:1, final drive 4.857:1.

DIMENSIONS: Length: 11ft 9in (3581mm); width: 5ft 0.25in (1530mm); height: 4ft 10in (1473mm); weight: 14cwt 2qtr 21lb (746kg); turning circle: 30ft 6in (9.3m).

CAPACITIES: Fuel 6 gallons (27 litres). Boot rear 25ft^3 (0.76m^3).

Below is the van version of the Imp: this was badged as a Commer.

Hillman Avenger

Introduced in early 1970 to compete with the likes of the Ford Escort and Vauxhall Viva, the Avenger fitted in between the Hunter and Imp ranges. Launched initially as a four-door saloon, an estate followed in early 1972, and a two-door saloon followed a year later in 1973. It was also sold in the USA as the Plymouth Cricket from 1971 to 1973. Engine upgrades came in 1973, it became a Chrysler model in 1976 with a styling update, and then a Talbot model in 1979; it was discontinued in 1981. There were no opening front quarter lights in the doors; instead there were dashboard mounted swivelling fresh air vents. Standard equipment (1970): heater with two-speed blower, screen washer, headlamp flasher, steering column lock, and more. Super adds: carpets, armrests, door pockets, centre console, reversing lights. GL as Super, plus twin headlights, two-speed wipers, reclining front seats, locking glovebox. Optional extras: radio, clock, cigarette lighter, reclining seats (standard on GL), seat belts, heated rear window, brake servo, automatic transmission, fog and spotlights, side repeater flashers, overriders, wing mirrors, and more.

COLOURS (1970-1974): Included Embassy black, Baltic blue, Carib blue, Oasis green, Safari beige, Tahiti beige, Firebrand red, Polar white, and metallics, Pewter, Silver mist, Phantom mist, Electric blue, Aquarios, Cedar green, Aztec gold, Tangerine, Sunset, Spice. GT model only: Firecracker, Sundance, Limelight.
ENGINE (at launch): All four-cylinder, OHV. Deluxe/Super: bore 78.6mm, stroke 64.3mm, 1248cc, maximum bhp 53 at 5000rpm, Stromberg 150CDS carburettor. GL: bore 86mm, stroke 64.3mm, capacity 1498cc, maximum bhp 63 at 5000rpm, Stromberg 150CDS carburettor. GT: as GL except maximum bhp 75 at 5000rpm, twin Stromberg 150CDS carburettors. Tiger, bore 87.4mm, stroke 66.7mm, 1598cc, maximum bhp 107 at 6100rpm, twin Weber carburettors.

1970 model specification

REAR AXLE: Semi-floating, hypoid bevel, ratios, 1248cc engine 4.375:1, 1498cc engine 3.889:1.

Instrument layout.

Deluxe/Super models.

GT/GLS models.

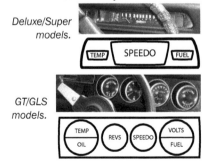

Red car above is an Avenger GT.

Gearbox ratios for Avenger models from 1970 to 1981

Rear axle: 4.375:1 **(1970-71 models)** top 4.375:1, 3rd 5.98:1, 2nd 8.88:1, 1st 14.26:1, reverse 15.01:1.

Rear axle: 4.375:1 **(later 1971 onwards)** top 4.375:1, 3rd 6.068:1, 2nd 9.472:1, 1st 15.479:1, reverse 16.1:1

Rear axle: 4.11:1, top 4.11:1, 3rd 5.701, 2nd 8.898:1, 1st 14.541:1, reverse 15.125:1

Rear axle: 3.889 (1970-71 models) top 3.889:1, 3rd 5.312:1, 2nd 7.89:1, 1st 12.9:1, reverse 13.42:1

Rear axle: 3.889 (later 1971 onwards) top 3.889:1, 3rd 5.394:1, 2nd 8.42:1, 1st 13.759:1, reverse 14.312:1

Rear axle: 3.7:1, top 3.7:1, 3rd 5.132:1, 2nd 8.01:1, 1st 13.09:1, reverse 13.62:1

Rear axle: 3.545:1, top 3.545:1, 3rd 4.91:1, 2nd 7.66:1, 1st 12.52:1, reverse 13.03:1

1970 model specification

BRAKES: Girling, front 9.5in discs, rear 8in drums, optional power assistance.

TYRES: Deluxe/Super/GL 5.60 x 13, GT 155 x 13.

SUSPENSION: Front MacPherson strut, coil springs and telescopic dampers, rear independent coil springs and trailing links with telescopic shock absorbers.

STEERING: Rack and pinion.

1970 model specification

DIMENSIONS: Length: saloon 13ft 5.4in (4100mm), estate 13ft 9.5in (4202mm); **width:** 5ft 2.5in (1588mm); **height:** 4ft 8in (1422mm); **weight:** Deluxe four-door saloon, 16cwt 3qtr 8lb (855kg), Super four-door saloon, 16cwt 3qtr 16lb (858kg), GL, 17cwt 10lb (868kg), Deluxe 1248cc estate, 18cwt 26lb (925kg), Super 1248cc estate, 18cwt 1qtr 13lb (932kg); **turning circle:** 32ft (9.75m).

CAPACITIES: Fuel 9 gallons (41 litres). Boot: saloon, 19ft^3 (0.6m^3), estate, maximum 60ft^3 (1.8m^3).

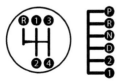

Floor-mounted gear change layouts: manual on left, automatic on right.

Hillman Avenger (1973-1976)

Avenger engines were enlarged in 1973 to 1295cc and 1598cc, however, 1295cc-engined models now had drum brakes all round. 1974 range Deluxe/Super/GL models were available as estate, or two- and four-door saloons; GT models were two-door saloon only, and GLS were four-door saloon only. Standard equipment (1974) on all models: carpet, heated rear window, alternator, and radial ply tyres. Super adds: lockable glovebox, two-speed wipers and reversing lights. GL/GT/GLS in addition to Super: dipping rear view mirror, reclining front seats (not GT), and vinyl roof covering (not GL). Optional extras: radio, reclining front seats (standard on GL, GLS), seat belts, brake servo (standard on GT, GLS), automatic transmission (only with 1600 engine), front fog lights, and more.

ENGINE (from 1973): All four-cylinder, OHV. Deluxe/Super/GL: bore 78.6mm, stroke 66.67mm, 1295cc, maximum bhp 57 at 5000rpm, Stromberg 150CD3 or SUHS4/C carburettor. GT: as above except 69bhp at 5800rpm with twin Stromberg 150CD3 or single 175CD3 carburettors. Optional engine for Deluxe/Super/GL: bore 87.4mm, stroke 66.7mm, capacity 1598cc, maximum bhp 69 at 5000rpm, Stromberg 150CD3 carburettor. GLS (optional for GT): bore 87.4mm, stroke 66.7mm, capacity 1598cc, 81bhp at 5500rpm, twin Stromberg 150CD3 orsingle 175CD3 carburettors. Tiger: as GLS except, maximum bhp 107 at 6100rpm, twin Weber carburettors.

Top two cars are Avenger Tigers.

Although only the GT & GLS had a vinyl roof covering as standard, it was available as an optional extra on other models; see also how it was continued across the bottom of the rear window on later models, as seen on the car above, but not on the earlier four-door models.

1974 model specification

Note: for GEARBOX ratios, see 1970 model.

REAR AXLE: Semi-floating, hypoid bevel, ratios, 1295cc SC engine 4.375:1, 1598cc engine 3.89:1, 1295cc TC engine 4.11:1.

BRAKES: 1295cc engine, Girling, front and rear 8in drums. 1598cc engine, Girling, front 9.5in discs, rear 8in drums, optional power assistance (standard on GLS and GT).

TYRES: 155 x 13.

SUSPENSION: Front MacPherson strut, rear independent coil springs, all details as per earlier models.

STEERING: Rack and pinion.

DIMENSIONS: Length: saloon 13ft 5.4in (4100mm), estate 13ft 9.5in (4202mm); **width:** 5ft 2.5in (1588mm); **height:** 4ft 7.3in (1405mm); **weight:** Deluxe two-door saloon 16cwt 1qtr 21lb (835kg), Super two-door saloon, 16cwt 2qtr 4lb (840kg), GLS four-door saloon, 17cwt 2qtr 24lb (900kg), Super 1598cc estate, 18cwt 1qtr 7lb (930kg) *(note: automatics add 29lb (13.1kg))*; **turning circle:** 33ft (10m).

CAPACITIES: Fuel 10 gallons (45 litres). Boot: saloon 19ft³ (0.6m³), estate maximum 60ft³ (1.8m³).

Above: an Avenger GT.

Floor-mounted gear change layouts: manual on left; automatic on right.

Chrysler/Talbot Avenger

Introduced in 1976, this car featured a styling update with a new front grille incorporating the indicators at the side of the headlights instead of under the front bumper, and the rear lights were rearranged in a horizontal line. Also new was electronic ignition without condenser or breaker points. The 1976 range comprised DL, Super and GLS, revised in 1977 to LS/GL estate and two or four-door saloons and GLS four-door saloon. Following Peugeot's acquisition of Chrysler's European operations in 1979, the Avenger was re-badged as a Talbot. Standard equipment (1977): heater with two-speed blower, two-speed wipers, electric screen washer, headlamp flasher, heated rear window, hazard warning flashers, driver's door mirror, and more. GL adds: clock, centre console cubby box, front door pockets, reclining front seats, reversing lights, rear fog lamps, dipping rear view mirror, tailgate wash/wipe on the estate, and more. GLS in addition to LS/GL: vinyl covered roof, front fog lamps, tinted glass, and more. Optional extras (1978): all models, rear seat belts, laminated windscreen, automatic transmission, headlamp wash/wipe (not LS), metallic paint. LS (standard on others), reclining front seats, front headrests, reversing/rear fog lights, and more.

COLOURS (1977): Included Ermine white, Sunflower, Imperial red, Cherry, Autumn leaf, Walnut, Navy blue, Royal blue and metallics, Champagne, Gold dust, Copperbeech, Peppermint, Pinewood, Kingfisher, Steel grey.

The red car above is a special edition 'Top Hat' – this style of vinyl roof was used on the earlier two-door GT models.

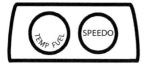

Instrument layout, DL model.
Note: indicator stalk now on left; on earlier Avengers it was on the right.

Instrument layout, GLS model.

COLOURS (1979): Included Ermine white, Cherry, Sweetcorn, Royal blue, Lagoon blue.
ENGINE: All four-cylinder, OHV. LS/GL: bore 78.6mm, stroke 66.67mm, 1295cc, maximum bhp 59 at 5000rpm, Stromberg 150CD3 or SU HS4C carburettor. Optional engine for LS/GL: bore 87.4mm, stroke 66.7mm, capacity 1598cc, maximum bhp 69 at 4800rpm, Stromberg 150CD3 or SU HS4C carburettor. GLS: as 1598cc above except 80bhp at 5400rpm with twin Stromberg 175CD carburettors.
GEARBOX: Four-speed, floor-mounted gear change, automatic transmission optional, synchromesh on all forward gears. Ratios: according to final drive (see earlier cars).
REAR AXLE: Semi-floating, hypoid bevel, ratios, 1295cc engine 3.889:1, 1598cc engine 3.545:1 From 1977, 1295cc Saloon 3.889:1, Estate 4.11:1, 1598cc Super saloon 3.545:1, GLS all models 3.7:1.
BRAKES: Girling, dual circuit, power assisted, front 9.5in discs, rear 8in drums.
TYRES: 155 x 13 (some later models 175 x 13).
SUSPENSION: Front MacPherson strut, coil springs and telescopic dampers, rear independent coil springs and trailing links with telescopic shock absorbers.
STEERING: Rack and pinion.
DIMENSIONS: Length: saloon (LS) 13ft 7.1in (4144mm), (GL/GLS) 13ft 8in (4166mm), estate (GL) 14ft 0.2in (4272mm); **width:** 5ft 3.5in (1615mm); **height:** saloon 4ft 7.3in (1405mm), estate 4ft 7.7in (1415mm); **weight:** LS two-door saloon 17cwt 1qtr 8lb (880kg), GLS four-door saloon 18cwt 1qtr (927kg), GL estate 18cwt 3qtr 14lb (959kg); **turning circle:** 33ft (10m).
CAPACITIES: Fuel 10 gallons (45 litres). Boot: saloon 19ft^3 (0.6m^3), estate maximum 60ft^3 (1.8m^3).

Floor gear change layouts: automatic left; manual right.

Talbot Avengers, identical in appearance to the Chrysler models but with Talbot badges instead of Chrysler, these were the last of the Avengers and were discontinued in 1981.

Humber Hawk mark 4

Introduced in 1950 with an enlarged engine of 2267cc and larger tyres, externally, only separate front sidelights readily identified the Hawk mark 4 from the mark 3. The Hawk name had originally been used for a Hillman model during the 1930s, and was subsequently used in 1946 on a Humber that had been derived from a Hillman model: the first true Humber Hawk being the mark 3 introduced in 1948. Optional extras included heater, radio, and overriders.

COLOURS: Black, Quartz blue, Pastel green, Satin bronze.
ENGINE: Four-cylinder, SV, bore 81mm, stroke 110mm, 2267cc, maximum bhp 58 at 3400rpm, Stromberg DBA36 carburettor.
GEARBOX: Four-speed, steering column gear change, synchromesh on top three gears. Ratios, top 4.55:1, 3rd 6.78:1, 2nd 11.24:1, 1st 16.19:1, reverse 21.62:1.
REAR AXLE: Hypoid bevel, ratio 4.55:1.
BRAKES: Lockheed front and rear 9in drums.
TYRES: 6.40 x 15.
SUSPENSION: Front independent with coil springs and wishbones, rear semi-elliptic leaf springs.
STEERING: Worm and nut.
DIMENSIONS: Length: 14ft 6in (4420mm); **width:** 5ft 10in (1778mm); **height:** 5ft 4in (1626mm); **weight:** approx 1 ton 4cwt 2qtr 14lb (1302kg, dry 1256kg).
CAPACITIES: Fuel 10 gallons (45 litres). Boot 15.5ft³ (4.8m³).

Note: increase in engine size over mark 3 from 1994cc to 2267cc, achieved by increasing bore from 77mm to 81mm.

Steering column gear change layout.

The car featured on this page has non-standard amber front and rear indicators. This is a common modification to many older cars.

Humber Hawk mark 5

Introduced in 1952 the mark 5 was mechanically identical to the mark 4 but had a lowered bonnet line, restyled front end with additional chrome, larger rear window and it was also longer. However, a 1953 Sales guide quotes the same boot capacity as the mark 4. The new Hawk was the basis for the new Super Snipe also launched in 1952. Optional extras: heater, radio, whitewall tyres, rim finishers.

COLOURS (1953): Black, Beech green, Gun, Quartz blue, Desert sand.
ENGINE: Four-cylinder, SV, bore 81mm, stroke 110mm, 2267cc, maximum bhp 58 at 3400rpm, Stromberg DAA36 carburettor.
GEARBOX: Four-speed, steering column gear change, synchromesh on top three gears. Ratios: top 4.55:1, 3rd 6.78:1, 2nd 11.24:1, 1st 14.5:1, reverse 18.037:1.
REAR AXLE: Semi-floating, hypoid bevel, ratio 4.55:1.
BRAKES: Lockheed front and rear 9in drums.
TYRES: 6.40 x 15.
SUSPENSION: Front independent with coil springs and wishbones, rear semi-elliptic leaf springs.
STEERING: Burman worm and nut.
DIMENSIONS: Length: 15ft 0.5in (4585mm); **width:** 5ft 10in (1778mm); **height:** 5ft 4.75in (1645mm); **weight:** 1 ton 6cwt 3qtr 7lb (1362kg); **turning circle:** 37ft (11.3m).
CAPACITIES: Fuel 10 gallons (45 litres). Boot 15.5ft^3 (4.8m^3).

Humber Hawk mark 6

Introduced in 1954, the mark 6 now had a front anti-roll bar and an overhead valve engine, a less powerful version of that fitted to the Sunbeam Talbot 90, but at 70bhp power was up from the previous Hawk side valve engine; it increased again to 75bhp with the introduction of the 6a in 1956. An estate was added to the range in 1955, it was the first time a Hawk estate had ever been available. Externally revised rear lights distinguished it from the mark 5. Standard equipment included a clock, two sun visors with mirror in passenger visor, front and rear central armrests, and front door pockets. Optional extras: heater and ventilation equipment, radio, individual front seats, screen washers, overdrive, fog lights, whitewall tyres, rim finishers, two-tone paint finish, and more.

COLOURS (1954): Black, Beech green, Desert sand, Quartz blue, Silver gun.
COLOURS (1956): Two-tone, Corinth blue/ Dawn mist, Pine green/Cactus green, Pearl grey/Mayfair grey, Pearl grey/Summer/blue. Single tones, Embassy black, Corinth blue, Cactus green, Mayfair grey.
ENGINE (mark 6): Four-cylinder, OHV, bore 81mm, stroke 110mm, 2267cc, maximum bhp 70 at 4000rpm, (mark 6a 75 at 4000rpm), Stromberg DI36 carburettor.
GEARBOX: Four-speed, steering column gear change, overdrive optional, synchromesh on

Instrument layout. Note: position of trafficator/ indicator switch on top of steering cowl is typical of 1950s cars.

The cars on this page are mark 6 saloons; the next page shows 6a saloons and estate, and the convertible is a 6.

top three gears. Ratios: o/d top 3.54:1, top 4.55:1, 3rd 6.79:1, 2nd 11.26:1, 1st 14.52:1, reverse 18.39:1.

REAR AXLE: Semi-floating, hypoid bevel, ratio 4.55:1 with or without overdrive.

BRAKES: Lockheed front and rear 10in drums.

TYRES: 6.40 x 15.

SUSPENSION: Front independent with coil springs and wishbones, rear semi-elliptic leaf springs, Armstrong shock absorbers all round.

STEERING: Burman worm and nut.

DIMENSIONS: Length: 15ft 1.5in (4610mm); **width:** 6ft (1829mm); **height:** 5ft 5in (1651mm); **weight:** 1 ton 8cwt 1qtr 16lb (1442kg); **turning circle:** 37ft (11.3m).

CAPACITIES: Fuel 10 gallons (45 litres).

Steering column gear change layout.

Humber Hawk series 1

Introduced in 1957, the Hawk series 1 was an all-new unitary construction design featuring distinctive two-tone paintwork, and a novel fuel filler incorporated into the rear light unit. The engine, however, was carried over from the mark 6a, but now had an automatic gearbox option. The fuel tank was subsequently increased to 12.5 gallons, and a genuine walnut wood dash replaced the simulated wood effect metal dash. An estate version was launched in October 1957. Standard equipment included a clock, lockable glovebox, front door pockets, two-speed wipers, and walnut trim. Optional extras: heater, radio, oil pressure gauge, ammeter, screen washers, individual reclining front seats, Laycock overdrive or Borg-Warner automatic transmission, whitewall tyres, rim finishers, and more.

COLOURS (1957) Estate: Two-tone, lower body and roof first, Cloud white/Airline blue, Antelope/Cloud white, Light Gun/Dawn mist, Iceberg green/Cypress green.

COLOURS (1958) Saloon: Two-tone, lower body and roof first, Corinth blue/Windsor blue, Glacier blue/Fathom grey, Embassy black/Thistle grey, Dawn mist/Seal grey, Burgundy/Cavalry beige.

ENGINE: Four-cylinder, OHV, bore 81mm, stroke 110mm, 2267cc, maximum bhp 78 at 4400rpm, Zenith WIA36 downdraught carburettor.

GEARBOX: Four-speed, steering column gear change, overdrive or automatic optional,

Instrument layout.

synchromesh on top three gears. Ratios: top 4.22:1, 3rd 6.297:1, 2nd 10.43:1, 1st 13.455:1, reverse 17.04:1.
REAR AXLE: Semi-floating, hypoid bevel, ratio 4.22:1.
BRAKES: Lockheed, power assisted, front 11in and rear 10in drums.
TYRES: 6.00 x 15 or 6.40 x 15.
SUSPENSION: Front independent with coil springs, rear semi-elliptic leaf springs, Armstrong telescopic shock absorbers all round.
STEERING: Burman recirculating ball.
DIMENSIONS: (series 1 and 1a) **Length:** 15ft 4.75in (4692mm); **width:** 5ft 9.5in (1765mm); **height:** saloon 5ft 1in (1549mm), estate 5ft 2in (1575mm); **weight:** saloon 1 ton 6cwt 2qtr (1346kg), estate 1 ton 9cwt 2qtr 7lb (1501kg); **turning circle:** 38ft (11.6m).
CAPACITIES (early series 1): Fuel 11.5 gallons (52 litres). Boot: saloon 19.5ft^3 (0.6m^3), estate 28ft^3 or 56ft^3 with rear seat folded down (0.8m^3 or 1.6m^3).

Steering column gear change layouts: manual on left; optional automatic on right.

Humber Hawk series 1a

Introduced in October 1959 with revised gear ratios and a different style of side trim, the Hawk would have to wait until 1960 before it gained the Super Snipe series 2 disc brakes, etc. Hawk brochures seem to show a narrow side stripe, like the saloon featured here, rather than the broader stripe used on the Super Snipe of the same period, and as also seen on a Hawk 1a estate exhibited at the NEC. Optional extras: heater, radio, individual front seats, Laycock overdrive or Borg-Warner automatic transmission, whitewall tyres, rim finishers, and more.

COLOURS (1959): Two-tone, main body colour first. Saloon: Foam white/ Haze blue, Biarritz blue/Haze blue, Windsor blue/ Embassy black, Glacier blue/Fathom grey, Slate blue/Ascot grey, Ascot grey/Burgundy, Smoke green/Sage green. Single tones, Foam white, Biarritz blue, Embassy black, Burgundy. Estate: Foam white/Windsor blue, Smoke green/Sage green, Slate blue/Ascot grey. Single tone, Slate blue.
ENGINE: Four-cylinder, OHV, bore 81mm, stroke 110mm, 2267cc, maximum bhp 78 at 4400rpm, Zenith WIA36 downdraught carburettor.
GEARBOX: Four-speed, steering column gear change, overdrive or automatic transmission optional, synchromesh on top three gears. Ratios: top 4.22:1, 3rd 5.877:1, 2nd 9.04:1, 1st 14.13:1, reverse 17.04:1; with overdrive, o/d top 3.54, top 4.55, 3rd 6.34, 2nd 9.75, 1st 15.25, reverse 19.31.
REAR AXLE: Semi-floating, hypoid bevel, ratio 4.22:1, with overdrive 4.55:1.
BRAKES: Lockheed, power assisted, front 11in and rear 10in drums.
TYRES: 6.00 x 15 or 6.40 x 15.
SUSPENSION: Front independent with coil springs, rear semi-elliptic leaf springs, Armstrong telescopic shock absorbers all round.
STEERING: Burman recirculating ball.
DIMENSIONS: See series 1.
CAPACITIES: Fuel 12.5 gallons (57 litres). Boot: saloon 19.5ft^3 (0.6m^3), estate 28ft^3 or 56ft^3 with rear seat folded down (0.8m^3 or 1.6m^3).

61

Humber Hawk series 2

Introduced in 1960, the series 2 featured front disc brakes, but lost its leather seats and automatic gearbox option. A point to note here is that whereas the Hawk became the 1a in 1959, the Super Snipe became the 2, hence the Hawk 2 here equates to the Super Snipe 3 and so on. 1961 retail price with overdrive £1311, the slightly smaller Rover 80 with overdrive cost £1438. Standard equipment included a heater and ventilator, clock, oil pressure gauge, ammeter, lockable glovebox, front door pockets, and screen washers. Optional extras: radio, individual front seats, seat belts, overdrive, fog lights, whitewall tyres, rim finishers.

COLOURS (1960): Saloon/estate: two-tone main body colour first, Charcoal/Dawn mist, Smoke green/Sage green, Foam white/Windsor blue, Biarritz blue/Windsor blue, Windsor blue/Embassy black (saloon only). Single tones (saloon), Embassy black, Biarritz blue, Smoke green, Burgundy. Single tones (estate), Charcoal, Smoke green.
ENGINE: Four-cylinder, OHV, bore 81mm, stroke 110mm, 2267cc, maximum bhp 78 at 4400rpm, Zenith WIA36 carburettor.
GEARBOX: Four-speed, steering column gear change, overdrive optional, synchromesh on top three gears. Ratios: top 4.22:1, 3rd 5.88:1, 2nd 9.04:1, 1st 14.16:1, reverse 17.89:1.
REAR AXLE: Semi-floating, hypoid bevel, ratio 4.22:1.
BRAKES: Girling, power assisted, front 11.38in discs, rear 11in drums.
TYRES: 6.00 x 15 or 6.40 x 15.
SUSPENSION: Front independent with coil springs, rear semi-elliptic leaf springs, Armstrong telescopic shock absorbers all round.
STEERING: Burman recirculating ball.
DIMENSIONS: Length: 15ft 4.75in (4692mm); **width:** 5ft 9.5in (1765mm); **height:** saloon 5ft 1in (1549mm), estate 5ft 2in (1575mm); **weight:** saloon 1 ton 7cwt 0qtr 27lb (1384kg), estate 1 ton 9cwt 1qtr 24lb (1497kg); **turning circle:** 38ft (11.6m).
CAPACITIES: See series 1a.

Note: overdrive switch is on right of steering column.

Instrument layout.

Humber Hawk series 3

The series 3 was introduced in 1962, with a mildly restyled rear window, improved steering, and an enlarged capacity petrol tank of 16 gallons. As previously mentioned, because the Hawk series numbering went from 1 to 1a and then 2, whereas the Super Snipe was simply 1 then 2 and so on, the series 3 Hawk featured here should always be compared to the series 4 Super Snipe, and not the series 3. The series 3 Hawk, with its distinctive rear window, is probably the easiest of the Hawks to recognise, however the rear end of the estate car remained unchanged, making it difficult to identify which series model any estate cars are. Standard equipment included a heater and ventilation equipment, clock, oil pressure gauge, ammeter, screen washers, synchromesh on all forward gears, and power assisted brakes. Optional extras: radio, cigar lighter, individual reclining front seats, seat belts, overdrive, wheel trim discs, and more.

COLOURS (1963): Saloon/estate: two-tone main body colour first, second is roof, Charcoal/Dawn mist, Smoke green/Sage green, Foam white/Windsor blue, Biarritz blue/Windsor blue. Single tones (saloon), Embassy black, Biarritz blue, Maroon, Smoke green. Single tones (estate), Charcoal, Smoke green.

ENGINE: Four-cylinder, OHV, bore 81mm, stroke 110mm, 2267cc, maximum bhp 78 at 4400rpm, Zenith WIA36-2 carburettor.

GEARBOX: Four-speed, steering column gear change, overdrive optional. Ratios: o/d top 3.28:1, top 4.22:1, o/d 3rd 4.57, 3rd 5.88:1, 2nd 9.04:1, 1st 14.16:1, reverse 17.89:1.

REAR AXLE: Semi-floating, hypoid bevel, ratio 4.22:1 with or without overdrive.

Some cars on these pages have been fitted with a stick-on heated rear screen demister – a popular accessory before the days of heated rear windows.

BRAKES: Girling, power assisted, front 11.38in discs, rear 11in drums.

TYRES: 6.40 x 15.

SUSPENSION: Front independent with coil springs, rear semi-elliptic leaf springs, Armstrong telescopic shock absorbers all round.

Left is a hub cap (nave plate) and rim finisher from the pre series 3 cars. Right is a wheel trim disc from series 3 cars onwards.

STEERING: Burman recirculating ball. **DIMENSIONS: Length:** 15ft 4.75in (4692mm); **width:** 5ft 9.5in (1765mm); **height:** saloon 5ft 1in (1549mm), estate 5ft 2in (1575mm); **weight:** saloon 1 ton 8cwt 1qtr 18lb (1443kg), estate 1 ton 10cwt 0qtr 11lb (1529kg); **turning circle:** 38ft (11.6m). **CAPACITIES:** Fuel 16 gallons (73 litres). Boot: saloon 19.5ft³ (0.6m³), estate 28ft³ or 56ft³ with rear seat folded down (0.8m³ or 1.6m³).

 Steering column gear change layout.

Note: handbrake by the side of driver's seat; a usual feature of Rootes cars in the 1960s.

Humber Hawk series 4 and 4a

Introduced in 1964 and discontinued in 1967, the series 4 had revised styling featuring a flat rear window and rear quarter lights, revised front sidelights and rear lights, new bumpers with rubber inserts in the overriders, the series 4a followed a year later in 1965 at which point the option of an automatic gearbox was reintroduced. Standard equipment as series 3 cars included full instrumentation, walnut trim, synchromesh on all forward gears, and power assisted brakes. Optional extras (1965): radio, cigar lighter, individual reclining front seats, seat belts, Laycock overdrive or Borg-Warner automatic transmission, wheel trim discs, and more.

COLOURS (1964): Saloon: Embassy black, Biarritz blue, Maroon, and metallics – Silver moss, Silver grey, Lavender grey, Burnt almond.
COLOURS (1965): Saloon: Embassy black, Maroon, and metallics – Silver moss, Silver grey, Lavender grey, Burnt almond, Royal blue. Estate: Charcoal, and metallics – Silver moss, Silver grey, Burnt almond, Royal blue.
ENGINE: Four-cylinder, OHV, bore 81mm, stroke 110mm, 2267cc, maximum bhp 78 at 4400rpm, Zenith WIA36-2 carburettor.
GEARBOX: Four-speed, steering column gear change, overdrive or automatic optional,

Instrument layout. Note: indicator stalk is on right; as was usual for most British cars during the 1960s.

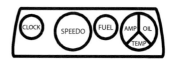

Hawks on this page are series 4; those on next page are series 4a.

Humbers are sometimes painted white for use as wedding cars.

synchromesh on all forward gears. Ratios:
o/d top 3.28:1, top 4.22:1, o/d 3rd 4.57:1,
3rd 5.88:1, 2nd 9.04:1, 1st 14.16:1, reverse
15.07:1.
REAR AXLE: Semi-floating, hypoid bevel, ratio
4.22:1 with or without overdrive or automatic
options.
BRAKES: Girling, power assisted, front
11.38in discs, rear 11in drums.
TYRES: 6.40 x 15.
SUSPENSION: Front independent with coil
springs, rear semi-elliptic leaf springs and anti-
roll bar, Armstrong telescopic shock absorbers
all round.
STEERING: Burman recirculating ball.

*Steering column gear
change layout.*

DIMENSIONS: Length: 15ft 4in (4673mm);
width: 5ft 10in (1778mm); **height:** saloon 4ft
11.25in (1505mm), estate 5ft 2in (1575mm);
weight: saloon 1 ton 8cwt 3qtr 22lb (1470kg),
estate 1 ton 10cwt 1qtr 2lb (1537kg); **turning
circle:** 38ft (11.6m).
CAPACITIES: Fuel 16 gallons (73 litres). Boot:
saloon 19.5ft³ (0.6m³), estate 28ft³ or 56ft³
with rear seat lowered, (0.8m³ or 1.6m³).

*Car above is fitted with earlier type front
sidelights.*

*Left: Front sidelights. Early
series Hawks top, later
models below.*

Humber Super Snipe mark 4/4a

Introduced in 1952, this was the first true postwar Super Snipe, with a new chassis, an extended version of the Hawk design to accommodate the new OHV engine of 4139cc developing 113bhp. This engine was uprated to 116bhp with the mark 4a and 130bhp with the 4b by raising the compression ratio. The 4a introduced in October 1953 featured full length strips on the front doors, as before it was available as a saloon or touring limousine with glass division, walnut trim was added in April 1954. Optional extras: heater and ventilation equipment, radio, and more.

COLOURS (1953): Black, Crystal green, Gun, Light fawn, Alpine Mist, Adriatic blue, Maroon.
COLOURS (1954): Black, Seal grey, Claret, Island mist, Baltic blue.

The convertible featured on this page was used by the Queen during her 1954 tour of Australia. Humbers and other Rootes cars were used for a number of Royal tours.

Earlier Super Snipes had been successfully used in rallies, taking 2nd place in the 1950 Monte Carlo, and completing the 15 countries in 90 hours event in 1952. However, it was the Sunbeam Talbot cars that were more frequently used in competitions during the 1950s.

ENGINE (4a): Six-cylinder, OHV, bore 88.9mm, stroke 111.13mm, 4139cc, maximum power 116bhp at 3600rpm, Stromberg DBVA42 carburettor.
GEARBOX: Four-speed, steering column gear change, synchromesh on all forward gears. Ratios (4.1:1 rear axle): top 4.1:1, 3rd 5.822:1, 2nd 8.577:1, 1st 12.808:1, reverse 3.579:1; ratios (3.7:1 rear axle): top 3.7:1, 3rd 5.255:1, 2nd 7.742:1, 1st 11.557:1, reverse 12.254:1; ratios (3.9:1 rear axle): top 3.9:1, 3rd 5.539:1, 2nd 8.161:1, 1st 12.182:1, reverse 12.917:1.
REAR AXLE: Three-quarter floating, hypoid bevel, mark 4 and early 4a cars 3.9 or 3.7, ratios later mark 4a cars 4.1:1 or 3.7:1.
BRAKES: Lockheed front and rear 11in drums.
TYRES: 7.00 x 15.
SUSPENSION: Front independent with coil springs, rear semi-elliptic leaf springs with Munroe telescopic shock absorbers all round.

The convertible at the top of the page is a mark 4; the car on the left is a mark 4a.

Steering column gear change layout.

STEERING: Burman worm and nut.
DIMENSIONS: Length: 16ft 5in (5004mm);
width: 6ft 1.5in (1867mm); **height:** 5ft 6in
(1676mm); **weight:** 1 ton 15cwt 3qtr 20lb
(1825kg); **turning circle:** 40ft (12.2m).
CAPACITIES: Fuel 15 gallons (68 litres).

Instrument layout.

Humber Super Snipe mark 4b

Introduced in 1955, the 4b can be
distinguished by its flush-fitting rear
number plate holder, and chrome strip just
under the door and rear windows. It was
discontinued in 1958. Standard equipment
included a clock, oil pressure gauge,
ammeter, walnut veneer trim, leather seats,
front bench seat adjustable for reach,
height and rake, and rim finishers. Optional
extras: heater and ventilation equipment,
radio, Laycock overdrive (from 1955),
Borg-Warner automatic transmission (from
1956), individual front seats (only with
automatic transmission), two-tone paint,
and more.

*The car in the top two pictures features
separate sidelights mounted on top of the
front wings, amber indicators in place of the
normal combined sidelights/indicators, with
white lens included in the front grill trim. This
conversion is the same as the normal sidelight
and indicator arrangement used on the Austin
A35 that was launched in 1956, perhaps the
source of this car's lights.*

COLOURS (1956): Two-tones, lower body
colour first, Biarritz blue/Thistle grey, Thistle
grey/Biarritz blue, Mayfair grey/Pearl grey,
Tyrolean green/Forest green. Single tones,
Embassy black, Thistle grey, Mayfair grey,
Maroon.
ENGINE: Six-cylinder, OHV, bore 88.9mm,
stroke 111.13mm, 4139cc, maximum power
130.5bhp at 3600rpm, Stromberg DBVA42
carburettor.

GEARBOX: Four-speed, overdrive or automatic
optional, synchromesh on all forward gears.
Ratios: o/d top 3.19:1, top 4.1:1, 3rd 5.822:1,
2nd 12.808:1, 1st 13.579:1, reverse

Steering column gear change layout.

The two middle cars on page 68 have been fitted with amber rear indicators (see above), albeit in different positions. The more usual rear light arrangement seen on the Super Snipe mark cars is shown on the grey car (bottom, page 68, and above left).

13.579:1; with automatic transmission, top 3.7:1, 2nd 5.31:1, 1st 8.53:1.
REAR AXLE: Three-quarter floating, hypoid bevel, ratios 4.1 with or without overdrive, 3.7 with optional automatic transmission.
BRAKES: Lockheed front and rear 11in drums.
TYRES: 7.00 x 15.
SUSPENSION: Front independent with coil springs, rear semi-elliptic leaf springs with Munroe telescopic shock absorbers all round.
STEERING: Burman worm and nut.
DIMENSIONS: Length: 16ft 5in (5004mm); **width:** 6ft 1.5in (1867mm); **height:** 5ft 6in (1676mm); **weight:** 1 ton 15cwt 3qtr 20lb (1825kg); **turning circle:** 40ft (12.2m).
CAPACITIES: Fuel 15 gallons (68 litres).

Humber Super Snipe series 1

Introduced in 1958, the series 1 was an entirely new design based on the 1957 Hawk. Unlike the Hawk, however, the engine was not carried over from the previous model, the Super Snipe 4139cc engine was replaced by a new 2651cc engine, developed by Armstrong Siddeley. The Super Snipe series 1 range consisted of a saloon, an estate, and a touring limousine with a wind-down partition. Standard equipment included a heater, leather front and rear bench seats with two folding tables located in the rear of the front seat squab, power assisted brakes, and full wheel covers. Optional extras: radio, individual front seats, power assisted steering, Laycock overdrive or Borg-Warner automatic transmission, whitewall tyres, and more.

COLOURS (1958): Two-tone, lower body and roof first. Saloon: Smoke green/Sage green, Seal grey/Dawn mist, Embassy black/Windsor blue, Fathom grey/Glacier blue. Single tones, Embassy black, Burgundy, and metallics – Grey, Blue. Estate: Sage green/Smoke green, Seal grey/Dawn mist. Single tone, Grey metallic only.
ENGINE: Six-cylinder, OHV, bore 82.55mm, stroke 82.55mm, 2651cc, maximum bhp 112 at 5000rpm, Stromberg DIV42 carburettor.

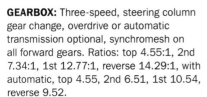

Above: rear lights and overriders. Series 1 to 4 on the left, series 5 and 5a on the right.

GEARBOX: Three-speed, steering column gear change, overdrive or automatic transmission optional, synchromesh on all forward gears. Ratios: top 4.55:1, 2nd 7.34:1, 1st 12.77:1, reverse 14.29:1, with automatic, top 4.55, 2nd 6.51, 1st 10.54, reverse 9.52.

REAR AXLE: Semi-floating, hypoid bevel, ratio 4.55:1 with or without automatic.

BRAKES: Girling, power assisted, front and rear 11in drums.

Steering column gear change layouts, manual on left, optional automatic on right.

Super Snipe rear windows: left, series 1, 2, 3; middle, 4; right, 5 and 5a.

TYRES: 6.70 x 15.
SUSPENSION: Front independent with coil springs, rear semi-elliptic leaf springs, Armstrong telescopic shock absorbers all round.
STEERING: Burman recirculating ball, power assistance optional.
DIMENSIONS: Length: 15ft 4.75in (4693mm); **width:** 5ft 9.5in (1765mm); **height:** saloon 5ft 1in (1549mm), estate 5ft 2in (1575mm); **weight:** estate 1 ton 10cwt 3qtr 12lb (1568kg); **turning circle:** 38ft (11.6m).
CAPACITIES: Fuel 12.5 gallons (57 litres). Boot: saloon 19.5ft³ (0.6m³), estate 28ft³ or 56ft³ with seat lowered, (0.8 or 1.6m³).

Humber Super Snipe series 2

The series 2 was introduced in 1959 with an enlarged engine of 2965cc, uprated suspension and front disc brakes. There was also a revised style of side trim similar to that used on the 1959 Singer Gazelle. Standard equipment included a heater, clock, oil pressure gauge, ammeter, walnut dash and door trim, two folding tables for rear passengers, screen washers, and power assisted brakes. Optional extras: radio, individual front seats, power assisted steering, Laycock overdrive or Borg-Warner automatic transmission, whitewall tyres, and more.

COLOURS (1959): Two-tone, main body colour first. Saloon: Biarritz blue/Haze blue, Foam white/Haze blue, Ascot grey/Burgundy, Smoke green/Sage green, Windsor blue/Embassy black, Glacier blue/Fathom grey, Slate blue/ Ascot grey (Charcoal/Dawn mist). Single tones, Embassy black, Burgundy, Biarritz blue, Foam white, (Smoke green, later models). Estate: Foam white/Windsor blue, Smoke green/Sage green, Slate blue/Ascot grey (Charcoal/Dawn mist), Single tone, Slate blue (Charcoal). *(Note: Charcoal colour schemes in brackets replaced earlier Slate blue schemes, see estate cars on following two pages for examples of both.)*

Instrument layout. Car shown on the left is an automatic.

ENGINE: Six-cylinder, OHV, bore 87.3mm, stroke 82.55mm, 2965cc, maximum bhp 129.5 at 4800rpm, Zenith 42WIA carburettor.
GEARBOX: Three-speed, steering column gear change, overdrive or automatic optional, synchromesh on all forward gears. Ratios: top 4.55:1, 2nd 7.34:1, 1st 12.77:1, reverse 14.29:1.
REAR AXLE: Semi-floating, hypoid bevel, ratio 4.55:1.
BRAKES: Girling, power assisted, front 11.38in discs, rear 11in drums.
TYRES: 6.70 x 15.
SUSPENSION: Front independent with coil springs and wishbones, rear semi-elliptic leaf springs, Armstrong telescopic shock absorbers all round.
STEERING: Burman recirculating ball, power assistance optional.
DIMENSIONS: Length: 15ft 4.75in (4693mm); **width:** 5ft 9.5in (1765mm); **height:** saloon 5ft 1in (1549mm); **weight:** saloon 1 ton 9cwt 3qtr 19lb (1520kg); **turning circle:** 38ft (11.6m).
CAPACITIES: Fuel 12.5 gallons (57 litres). Boot: saloon 19.5ft^3 (0.6m^3), estate 28 or 56ft^3 with seat lowered (0.8 or 1.6m^3).

Humber Super Snipe series 3

Introduced in 1960, this model had new front end styling with four headlights. It is interesting to note that some series 3 cars have white front indicator lens as used on the series 2 models, whilst some have amber lens as seen on the series 4 cars. The Humber Hawk did not have amber front indicators fitted until 1964. Although Rootes rally cars usually came from the Sunbeam stable, Sunbeam Talbot, Alpine and Rapier, the Super Snipe was also occasionally used, achieving 1st in class in the 1961 RAC rally, finishing 4th overall in the 1962 East African Rally (in which only 38 of the original 77 cars finished), and taking 2nd in class in the 1964 Circuit of Ireland. Standard equipment included a heater, clock, oil pressure gauge, ammeter, water temperature gauge, cigarette lighter, two folding tables for rear seat passengers, and power assisted brakes. Optional extras: radio, reclining front seats, seat belts, anti-condensation panel for rear window, power steering, Laycock overdrive or Borg-Warner automatic transmission, fog and spotlights, wing mirrors, tow hook, roof rack. *(Note: throughout the book, amongst the optional extras, some items have been included that are recorded on Rootes brochures as Accessories, and which would be fitted at the dealers, not the factory, eg: radio, fog and spotlights, wheel trims, wing mirrors, tow hook, roof rack.)*

COLOURS (1961): Saloon/estate: two-tone, main body colour first, second is roof, Charcoal/Dawn mist, Smoke green/Sage green, Biarritz blue/Windsor blue, Foam white/Windsor blue, Windsor blue/Embassy black (saloon only). Single tones (saloon and estate), Charcoal, Smoke green. Saloon only, Embassy black, Burgundy, Biarritz blue, Foam white.

ENGINE: Six-cylinder, OHV, bore 87.3mm, stroke 82.55mm, 2965cc, maximum bhp 129.5 at 4800rpm, Zenith 42WIA carburettor.
GEARBOX: Three-speed, steering column gear change, overdrive or automatic transmission optional, synchromesh on all forward gears. Ratios: o/d top 3.54:1, top 4.55:1, o/d 2nd 5.71:1, 2nd 7.34:1, 1st 12.77:1, reverse 14.29:1; with automatic, top 4.22, 2nd 6.04, 1st 9.75, reverse 8.82.
REAR AXLE: Semi-floating, hypoid bevel, ratio with or without overdrive 4.55:1, automatic 4.22:1.
BRAKES: Girling, power assisted, front 11.38in discs, rear 11in drums.
TYRES: 6.70 x 15.
SUSPENSION: Front independent with coil springs and wishbones, rear semi-elliptic leaf springs, Armstrong telescopic shock absorbers all round.
STEERING: Burman recirculating ball, power assistance optional.
DIMENSIONS: Length: 15ft 8in (4775mm); **width:** 5ft 9.5in (1765mm); **height:** saloon 5ft 1in (1549mm); **weight:** saloon 1 ton 9cwt 3qtr 26lb (1523kg, dry 1466kg), estate 1 ton 10cwt 3qtr 19lb (1571kg, dry 1514kg); **turning circle:** 38ft (11.6m).
CAPACITIES: Fuel 12.5 gallons (57 litres). Boot: saloon 19.5ft^3 (0.6m^3), estate 28ft^3 or 56ft^3 with seat lowered (0.8 or 1.6m^3).

Steering column gear change layouts, manual on left, optional automatic on right.

Humber Super Snipe series 4

Introduced in 1962, the series 4 featured a mildly revised rear window, opening rear quarter lights and 16 gallon fuel tank. The estate retained the rear end styling of all previous series Super Snipes. 1962 retail price £1481. (A Rover 3-litre cost £1668). Standard equipment included heater, clock, oil pressure gauge, ammeter, water temperature gauge, cigarette lighter, two folding tables for rear passengers, and power assisted brakes. Optional extras: radio, reclining front seats, seat belts, power steering, Laycock overdrive or Borg-Warner automatic transmission, auxiliary lights, whitewall tyres, and more.

COLOURS (1963): Saloon/estate: two-tone, main body colour first, second is roof, Charcoal/Dawn Mist, Smoke green/Sage green, Foam white/Windsor blue, Biarritz blue/Foam white. Single tones (saloon and estate), Charcoal, Smoke green, Sapphire blue, Silver grey metallic. Saloon only, Embassy black, Biarritz blue, Maroon, Foam white. Note, Embassy black was available throughout the life of the Super Snipe series cars and Smoke green/Sage green until two-tones were discontinued.

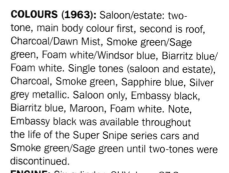

ENGINE: Six-cylinder, OHV, bore 87.3mm, stroke 82.55mm, 2965cc, maximum bhp 132 at 5000rpm, Zenith 42WIA carburettor.
GEARBOX: Three-speed, steering column gear change, overdrive or automatic transmission optional, synchromesh on all forward gears. Ratios: top 4.22:1, 2nd 6.129:1, 1st 11.835:1, reverse 13.25:1, with automatic, top 4.22, 2nd 6.03, 1st 9.77, reverse 8.82.
REAR AXLE: Semi-floating, hypoid bevel, ratio 4.22:1 with or without automatic.
BRAKES: Girling, power assisted, front 11.38in discs, rear 11in drums.

TYRES: 6.70 x 15.
SUSPENSION: Front independent with coil springs and wishbones, rear semi-elliptic leaf springs, Armstrong telescopic shock absorbers all round.
STEERING: Burman recirculating ball.

DIMENSIONS: Length: 15ft 8in (4775mm); **width:** 5ft 9.5in (1765mm); **height:** saloon 5ft 1in (1549mm), estate 5ft 2in (1575mm); **weight:** saloon 1 ton 10cwt 3qtr (1562kg); **turning circle:** 38ft (11.6m).
CAPACITIES: Fuel 16 gallons (73 litres). Boot: saloon 19.5ft^3 (0.6m^3), estate 28ft^3 or 56ft^3 with seat lowered (0.8 or 1.6m^3).

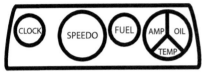

Instrument layout.

Models on this page are series 5, those on following page are series 5a. Imperial models top half of pages, Super Snipes below.

Humber Super Snipe series 5 and 5a

Introduced in 1964 with revised styling, series 5 and 5a featured the flat rear window found across the Rootes range, it also had revised rear lights, more engine power and power steering. An upmarket model called the Imperial was also introduced, which featured a vinyl roof covering. The series 5a with alternator and negative earth electrics followed in 1965 – the Police had some 5a cars supplied with positive earth electrics. Early Imperials featured the Super Snipe logo on the boot, later models had Imperial lettering. Both Super Snipe and Imperial were discontinued in 1967. Standard equipment on Humber Imperial: push button radio with rear compartment speakers with independent volume control, front and rear heating/ventilation, heated rear window, foldaway tables and reading lamps in rear, fog and spotlight, warning lights on edges of doors, variable rear shock absorbers. Standard equipment on Super Snipe: heater and ventilation equipment, two foldaway tables for passengers in rear, walnut trim, power assisted steering, and more. Optional extras for saloon and estate: radio, individual reclining front seats, seat belts, Laycock overdrive or Borg-Warner automatic transmission, and more.

COLOURS (1965) Imperial: Embassy black, Maroon, and metallics – Silver grey, Glade green, Royal blue.
COLOURS (1964) Super Snipe saloon: Embassy black, Biarritz blue, Maroon, Foam white, and metallics – Silver moss, Silver grey, Lavender grey, Burnt almond.
COLOURS (1965) Estate: Charcoal, and metallics – Silver moss, Silver grey, Burnt almond, Royal blue.
ENGINE: Six-cylinder, OHV, bore 87.3mm, stroke 82.55mm, 2965cc, maximum bhp 137 at 5000rpm, twin Stromberg 175CD carburettors.

Automatic gear change layout as used on the series 5 models; see next page for 5a model.

*Instrument layout.
Car shown on right
has overdrive.*

GEARBOX: Three-speed, steering column gear change, overdrive or automatic optional, synchromesh on all forward gears. Ratios: o/d top 3.28, top 4.22:1, 2nd 6.13:1, 1st 11.84:1, reverse 13.25:1, with automatic, top 4.22, 2nd 6.04, 1st 9.75, reverse 8.82.

Steering column gear change layouts, manual on left, optional automatic on right.

REAR AXLE: Semi-floating, hypoid bevel, ratio 4.22:1 with or without overdrive or automatic.
BRAKES: Girling, power assisted, front 11.38in discs, rear 11in drums.
TYRES: 6.70 x 15.
SUSPENSION: Front independent with coil springs and wishbones, rear semi-elliptic leaf springs, Armstrong telescopic shock absorbers all round.
STEERING: Burman recirculating ball, power assisted.
DIMENSIONS: Length: 15ft 7.5in (4763mm); **width:** 5ft 10in (1778mm); **height:** saloon 4ft 11.75in (1518mm), estate 5ft 2in (1575mm); **weight:** saloon 1 ton 11cwt 3qtr 15lb (1620kg), estate 1 ton 12cwt 2qtr 10lb (1656kg); **turning circle:** 38ft (11.6m).
CAPACITIES: Fuel 16 gallons (73 litres). Boot: saloon 19.5ft³ (0.6m³), estate 28ft³ or 56ft³ with rear seat lowered (0.8m³ or 1.6m³).

Humber Sceptre mark 1

Introduced in 1963, over a year later than its Super Minx and Vogue counterparts, the Sceptre was originally intended to replace the Rapier, but just as the Minx and Gazelle remained, so did the Rapier, and the Sceptre became part of the Humber range instead. A Solex carburettor replaced the twin Zeniths shortly after launch in 1963, and overriders with rubber inserts; an all-synchromesh gearbox, and fully reclining front seats followed in 1964. Ultimately, the fuel filler was changed to the style used on the mark 2 Sceptre. Examples of cars showing all the various external changes are included here. Standard equipment included heater and ventilation system with blower, clock, oil pressure gauge, ammeter, revolution counter, screen washers, headlamp flasher, Laycock overdrive, reversing lights, overriders, wheel trim discs, and more. Optional extras: radio, seat belts, whitewall tyres, two-tone paint, and more.

COLOURS (1963): Two-tones, lower body colour first, Pippin red/Pearl grey, Velvet green/Sage green, Quartz blue metallic/Moonstone, Solent blue metallic/Moonstone, Moonstone/Quartz blue metallic. Single tones, Pippin red, and metallics – Quartz blue, Solent blue, Bronze.

Instrument layout.

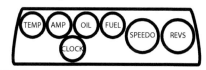

This page, top three photos: early models with large chrome overriders. Bottom two photos, and top half of next page: mid season models with rubber inserts in overriders. Lower half of next page: later models with Sceptre mark 2 type petrol filler cap.

ENGINE: Four-cylinder, OHV, bore 81.5mm, stroke 76.2mm, 1592cc, maximum bhp 85.5 at 5200rpm, twin Zenith 36WIA3 carburettors (later cars Solex 32PAIA).
GEARBOX: Four-speed, floor-mounted gear change with overdrive on top and third, synchromesh on top three gears. Ratios: o/d top 3.39:1, top 4.22:1, o/d 3rd 4.72:1, 3rd 5.88:1, 2nd 9.04:1, 1st 14.13:1, reverse 17.89:1.
REAR AXLE: Semi-floating, hypoid bevel, ratio 4.22:1.
BRAKES: Lockheed, power assisted, front 9.75in discs, rear 9in drums.
TYRES: 6.00 x 13.
SUSPENSION: Front independent coil springs and swinging links, anti-roll bar, rear semi-elliptic leaf springs, telescopic shock absorbers all round.
STEERING: Burman recirculating ball.
DIMENSIONS: Length: 13ft 9.5in (4203mm); **width:** 5ft 3.25in (1607mm); **height:** 4ft 9in (1448mm); **weight:** 1 ton 1cwt 3qtr 19lb (1113kg); **turning circle:** 36ft (10.9m).
CAPACITIES: Fuel 10.5 gallons (48 litres). Boot capacity 16ft³ (0.5m³).

Floor gear change layout.

Both colour schemes shown here are from mid-season models, with rubber inserts in overriders, and original petrol filler cap. So, which is correct – or was there a styling change during production of the mid-season models?

Below: late models with mark 2 type fuel filler cap.

Left: fuel filler flap for early Sceptre mark 1, Hillman Super Minx and Singer Vogue mark 1 and 2. Right: locking fuel cap for later Sceptre mark 1, Hillman Super Minx and Singer Vogue mark 3 and 4.

Humber Sceptre mark 2

Introduced in 1965 with an enlarged engine of 1725cc, the Sceptre mark 2 adopted the front wings and bonnet style of the Super Minx instead of the Vogue style; the rear of the car, however, remained unchanged, although the Super Minx and Vogue had been restyled a year earlier. It should be noted that, from the start, the Sceptre had a lower rear roof line and different rear wings from the Super Minx and Vogue. An alternator was now fitted instead of a dynamo, and automatic transmission was available as an option, but gone was the option of a two-tone paint scheme. Standard equipment included heater and ventilation system with blower, clock, oil pressure gauge, ammeter, revolution counter, screen washer, headlamp flasher,

Note: detailed differences between mark 1 and 2 models – ie, see how the grille forms part of the bonnet on the mark 1 (left).

reclining front seats, adjustable telescopic steering column, overdrive, reversing lights, overriders, alternator. Optional extras: radio, seat belts, Borg-Warner automatic transmission, whitewall tyres, and more.

COLOURS (1965): Pippin red, and metallics – Quartz blue, Royal blue, Glade green, Sherwood green, Autumn gold, Silver grey.
ENGINE: Four-cylinder, OHV, bore 81.5mm, stroke 82.55mm, 1725cc, maximum bhp 91 at 5500rpm, Solex B32PAIAS twin choke carburettor.
GEARBOX: Four-speed, floor-mounted gear change with overdrive on top and third gears, automatic optional, synchromesh on all forward gears. Ratios: o/d top 3.39:1, top 4.22:1, o/d 3rd 4.72:1, 3rd 5.88:1, 2nd 9.04:1, 1st 14.18:1, reverse 15.07:1.
REAR AXLE: Semi-floating, hypoid bevel, ratio 4.22:1.
BRAKES: Lockheed, power assisted, front 10.3in discs, rear 9in drums.
TYRES: 6.00 x 13.
SUSPENSION: Front independent coil springs and swinging links, rear semi-elliptic leaf springs, telescopic shock absorbers all round.

Hillman Super Minx on left has indentation on rear wing just wide enough to accommodate rear lights, whereas Humber Sceptre on right has indentation extending across to boot lid and also has a ridge with trim along top of wing.

Floor gear change layout.

STEERING: Burman recirculating ball with adjustable telescopic steering column.
DIMENSIONS: Length: 13ft 11in (4242mm); **width:** 5ft 3.25in (1607mm); **height:** 4ft 9in (1448mm); **weight:** 1 ton 1cwt 2qtr 7lb (1095kg); **turning circle:** 36ft (10.9m).
CAPACITIES: Fuel 10.5 gallons (48 litres). Boot capacity 16ft³ (0.5m³).

Humber Sceptre mark 3

Introduced in 1967, this was the ultimate model in the Arrow range, combining the performance of the Rapier with the luxury of the Vogue. Like the rest of the Arrow range it featured MacPherson strut suspension with front anti-roll bar. For 1974 the optional three-speed automatic was replaced by a four-speed,

Note: cars on this page are early models and those on next two pages are later models (see above for differences).

Instrument layout.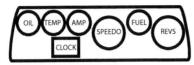

this was followed later in the year by a restyle, featuring revised bumpers and rear panel, and with fitment of additional equipment as standard. An estate model was also introduced at this time. Chrysler discontinued the Humber Sceptre range in 1976, all other Humbers having already been discontinued in 1967. Standard equipment at launch included heater/ ventilation equipment with two-speed blower, clock, oil pressure gauge, ammeter, revolution counter, two cigar lighters, full-length front console, fully reclining front seats, rear seat centre armrest and cubby box, two-speed wipers, screen washer, Laycock overdrive, reversing lights, vinyl roof covering (saloons only), overriders and wheel cover discs. Optional extras: radio, Borg-Warner automatic transmission, fog and spotlights, whitewall tyres, and more.

COLOURS (1967): All with black vinyl roof covering. Prussian blue, and metallics – Laurel green, Gunmetal, Aqua, Golden sand, Claret.
COLOURS (1975): All saloons with black vinyl roof covering. Polar white, Cherry, Magenta, Imperial red, Sunflower, Apricot, Orange blossom, Lavender, Carib blue, and metallics – Peppermint, Pinewood, Copperbeech, Champagne, Kingfisher.
ENGINE: Four-cylinder, OHV, bore 81.5mm, stroke 82.5mm, 1725cc, maximum bhp 94 at 5200rpm, twin Stromberg 150CDS variable choke carburettors, (later cars twin Stromberg 150CD3).
GEARBOX: Four-speed, floor-mounted gear change with overdrive on top and third gears, automatic transmission optional, synchromesh on all forward gears. Ratios: o/d top 3.12:1, top 3.89:1, o/d 3rd 4.35:1, 3rd 5.41:1, 2nd 8.32:1, 1st 13.04:1, reverse 13.88:1.

Floor gear change layouts, manual on left and optional automatic on right.

REAR AXLE: Semi-floating hypoid bevel, ratio 3.89:1, (3.7:1 with automatic transmission).
BRAKES: Lockheed, power assisted, front 9.6in discs, rear 9in drums.
TYRES: 6.00 x 13.

SUSPENSION: Front fully independent coil spring and strut, rear semi-elliptic leaf springs and telescopic shock absorbers.
STEERING: Burman recirculating ball with adjustable telescopic steering column.
DIMENSIONS: Length: early saloons 14ft 1.5in (4305mm), later saloons 14ft 3in (4343mm), estate 14ft 5in (4394mm); **width:** 5ft 3.5in (1613mm); **height:** saloon 4ft 8in (1422mm), estate 4ft 10in (1473mm) including standard fit roof rack; **weight:** saloon 19cwt 1qtr 2lb (991kg), estate 1 ton 3qtr 2lb (1055kg); **turning circle:** 33ft 6in (8.5m).
CAPACITIES: Fuel 10 gallons (45 litres). Boot: saloon 17ft^3 (0.5m^3), estate maximum 62ft^3 (1.8m^3).

Singer SM 1500

Produced from 1948 to 1954, the SM 1500 was the first post war Singer, and it was this vehicle, in face-lifted form and selling as the Singer Hunter, that was in production when Rootes acquired Singer in 1955. The 1954 retail price was £893. Standard equipment included heater, oil pressure gauge, ammeter, folding centre armrests in both front and rear seats, and more.

COLOURS (1953): Included Coronation blue, British green, Silver gunmetal, Black, all available as two-tones with Silver gunmetal upper panels for an additional £6 6s (£6.30).
ENGINE: Four-cylinder OHC in-line, early cars bore 73mm, stroke 90mm, capacity 1506cc, maximum bhp 48 at 4500rpm, single Solex 30FAI carburettor. From 1951, bore 73mm, stroke 89.4mm, capacity 1497cc, maximum bhp 48 at 4500rpm, or 58 at 4600rpm, twin Solex 30FAI carburettors.
GEARBOX: Four-speed, steering column gear change, synchromesh on top three gears. Ratios: top 5.125:1, 3rd 7.518:1, 2nd 11.633:1, 1st 18.4:1.
REAR AXLE: Hypoid bevel.

Instrument layout on early cars.

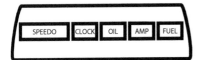

Steering column gear change layout.

During its life the SM 1500 was subject to a number of modifications/ improvements, such as revised bumpers (hence increase in overall length), and enlarged rear screen, as can be seen on the car on the right. Early car at top is fitted with non-standard amber indicators.

Instrument layout on later cars.

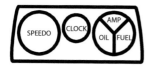

BRAKES: Lockheed, front and rear 9in drums.
TYRES: 5.50 x 16.
SUSPENSION: Front independent coil, rear
semi-elliptic leaf springs.
STEERING: Worm and nut.
DIMENSIONS: Length: 14ft 6in (4420mm),
later cars 14ft 9in (4496mm); **width:** 5ft
3in (1600mm); **height:** 5ft 4in (1626mm);
weight: 1 ton 4cwt 0qtr 12lb (1225kg);
turning circle: 33ft (10m).
CAPACITIES: Fuel 10 gallons (45 litres). Boot
13ft^3 (0.4m^3).

Singer Hunter

The Hunter was introduced in 1954 to replace
the SM 1500. During 1956 an S model was
produced, lacking the heater, fog lights, clock,
overriders, spare wheel, etc, of the standard
car. Standard equipment included, heater,
clock, ammeter, two sun visors, screen
washers, comprehensive tool kit, automatic
reversing light, twin fog lights, overriders, rim
finishers, twin horns, and more.
During 1955, just prior to the Rootes
takeover, Singer announced the Hunter 75.
Using a twin-cam engine with twin Solex
carburettors, it developed 75 bhp, however
Rootes quickly stopped production of it, and
very few were ever built.

COLOURS (1956): Two-tone, Black/Grey,
Coronation blue/Grey, British green/Grey.
Single tones, Grey, Black, Coronation blue,
British green.
ENGINE: Four-cylinder OHC in-line, bore
73mm, stroke 89.4mm, capacity 1497cc,
maximum bhp 48 at 4500rpm with single
Solex 30FAI carburettor (58bhp at 4600rpm,
twin Solex 30FAI carburettors).
GEARBOX: Four-speed, steering column or
floor-mounted gear change, synchromesh
on top three gears. Ratios: top 5.125:1,
3rd 6.95:1, 2nd 10.75:1, 1st and reverse
17.02:1.
REAR AXLE: Hypoid bevel, ratio 5.125:1.
BRAKES: Lockheed, front and rear 9in drums.
10in drums from 1956 with the Hunter 75.
TYRES: 5.50 x 16.
SUSPENSION: Front independent coil and
wishbones, rear semi-elliptic leaf springs.
STEERING: Worm and nut.

DIMENSIONS: Length: 14ft 9in (4496mm); **width:** 5ft 3in (1600mm); **height:** 5ft 4in (1626mm); **weight:** 1 ton 3cwt 2qtr 0lb (1193kg); **turning circle:** 33ft (10m). **CAPACITIES: Fuel** 10 gallons (45 litres). Boot 13ft³ (0.4m³).

Instrument layout.

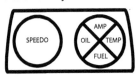

Note: handbrake on right of steering column.

Singer Gazelle series 1

Introduced in 1956 in saloon and convertible form, the Gazelle series 1 was the first Rootes Singer, and, like all Singers that followed, it was really an upmarket version of the Hillman model range; in this case the Minx series 1. Initially, Singer's own engines were used, and from the front or side they could be identified by their own unique styling. It was also a well equipped car with an oil pressure gauge, ammeter, and windscreen washers fitted as standard, and had a burr walnut finish dashboard and door trim. Optional extras: heater, radio, clock, individual front seats, whitewall tyres, and more.

COLOURS (1956): Two-tone, lower body colour first. Saloon: Corinth blue/Embassy black, Windsor blue/Corinth blue, Glacier blue/Fathom grey, Dawn mist/Shadow grey, Shadow grey/Burgundy. Single tones, Embassy black, Shadow grey, Windsor blue, Burgundy. Convertible: Summer blue/Dawn mist with blue hood, Embassy black/Pippin red with black hood, Embassy black/Tyrollean green with black hood, Pippin red/Pearl grey with red hood.
ENGINE: Four-cylinder SOHC, bore 73mm,

Instrument layout.

Steering column gear change layout.

stroke 89.4mm, 1496cc, maximum bhp 52.5 at 4500rpm, Solex 30FA10-2 carburettor.
GEARBOX: Four-speed, steering column gear change. Ratios: top 4.78:1, 3rd 7.13:1, 2nd 11.81:1, 1st 17.045:1, reverse 22.73:1.
REAR AXLE: Spiral bevel, ratio 4.78:1.
BRAKES: Lockheed, front and rear 9in drums.
TYRES: 5.60 x 15.
SUSPENSION: Front independent coil springs and wishbones, rear semi-elliptic leaf springs.
STEERING: Burman worm and nut.
DIMENSIONS: Length: 13ft 7.5in (4153mm); **width:** 5ft 0.75in (1543mm); **height:** saloon 4ft 11.5in (1511mm), convertible 4ft 10in (1473mm); **weight:** saloon 1 ton 0cwt 2qtr 4lb (1043kg), convertible 1 ton 0cwt 3qtr 6lb (1057kg); **turning circle:** 34ft 3in (10.4m).
CAPACITIES: Fuel 7.5 gallons (34 litres). Boot 13.5ft³ (0.4m³).

Singer Gazelle series 2

The series 2 was introduced in 1957 in saloon and convertible form to replace the series 1, to which it was mechanically identical. An estate car was added to the range in October 1957. The series 2 now had a 10 gallon fuel tank, and featured a side flash that would remain a characteristic of the model until the introduction of the Arrow range Gazelle in 1967. Standard equipment included overriders and windscreen washers, items that were options on many other vehicles! Optional extras: heater, radio, clock, individual front seats, overdrive, and more.

COLOURS (1957): Two-tone, main body colour first, second is side flash. Saloon: Embassy black/Thistle grey, Windsor blue/Cloud white, Glacier blue/Embassy black, Fathom grey/Glacier blue, Burgundy/Cavalry beige. Convertible: Embassy black/Thistle grey, Windsor blue/Cloud white, Glacier blue/Embassy black, Pippin red/Pearl grey, all with black hoods.

Note, car shown here has non-standard amber front indicators fitted in place of combined indicators and sidelights, and has then had non-standard sidelights mounted on top of front wings.

ENGINE (series 2): Four-cylinder SOHC, bore 73mm, stroke 89.4mm, 1496cc, maximum bhp 52.5 at 4500rpm, Solex 30FA10-2 carburettor.
GEARBOX: Four-speed, steering column gear change, overdrive optional. Ratios: o/d top 3.61:1, top 4.78:1, o/d 3rd 5.39:1, 3rd 7.13:1, 2nd 11.81:1, 1st 17.045:1, reverse 22.73:1.
REAR AXLE: Spiral bevel (series 2 and 2a), ratio 4.78:1 with or without overdrive.

1958 Series 2a specification
ENGINE (2a): Four-cylinder OHV, bore 79mm, stroke 76.2mm, 1494cc, maximum bhp 60 at 4500rpm, Solex PB10 carburettor.
GEARBOX (2a): Four-speed, steering column gear change, overdrive optional, synchromesh on top three gears. Ratios with overdrive: o/d top 3.61:1 top 4.78:1, o/d 3rd 5.39:1, 3rd 7.13:1, 2nd 11.81:1, 1st 15.22:1, reverse 19.29:1.

BRAKES: Lockheed, front and rear 9in drums.
TYRES: 5.60 x 15.
SUSPENSION: Front independent coil springs and wishbones, rear semi-elliptic leaf springs.
STEERING: Burman worm and nut, later recirculating ball.
DIMENSIONS: Length: 13ft 7.5in (4153mm); **width:** 5ft 0.75in (1543mm); **height:** saloon 4ft 11.5in (1511mm), convertible 4ft 10in (1473mm); **weight:** saloon 1 ton 1cwt 0qtr 8lb (1070kg), convertible 1 ton 1cwt 2qtr 12lb (1098kg); **turning circle:** 34ft 3in (10.4m).
CAPACITIES: Fuel 10 gallons (45 litres). Boot: saloon/convertible 13.5ft³ (0.4m³), estate 26ft³ or 44ft³ (0.8 or 1.32m³).

Singer Gazelle series 3

Introduced in 1958 to replace the short-lived series 2 and 2a, the Gazelle series 3 was becoming more like its Minx counterpart, having had its original Singer OHC engine replaced with the Minx unit. It did, however, retain its unique front grille and wood interior trim. Saloon, estate and convertible were available from the start. Standard equipment included oil pressure gauge, ammeter, windscreen washers, overriders, and rim finishers. Optional extras: heater, radio, clock, individual front seats, Laycock overdrive, reversing light, and more.

COLOURS (1958): Two-tone, main body colour first, second is side flash and estate roof. Saloon: Windsor blue/Cloud white, Fathom grey/Glacier blue, Burgundy/Cavalry beige, Embassy black/Windsor blue, Smoke green/Sage green.
Estate: Smoke green/Sage green, Windsor blue/Cloud white, Seal grey/Cloud white, Dawn mist/Seal grey. Convertible: Windsor blue/Cloud white with Corinth blue or black hood, Pippin red/Pearl grey with Pippin red or black hood, Embassy black/Windsor blue with black hood, Smoke green/Sage green with green hood.

Instrument layout.

ENGINE: Four-cylinder OHV, bore 79mm, stroke 76.2mm, 1494cc, maximum bhp 60 at 4500rpm, Solex 32PB10 carburettor.

GEARBOX: Four-speed, steering column gear change, overdrive optional, synchromesh on top three gears. Ratios: saloon/convertible top 4.55:1, 3rd 6.78:1, 2nd 11.24:1, 1st 14.50:1, reverse 18.37:1; saloon/convertible with overdrive and all estates with or without, o/d top 3.61, top 4.78, o/d 3rd 5.39, 3rd 7.13, 2nd 11.81, 1st 15.22, reverse 19.29.

REAR AXLE: Semi-floating, spiral bevel, ratio: saloon/convertible 4.55:1, with overdrive 4.78:1, estate 4.78:1 with or without overdrive.

BRAKES: Lockheed, front and rear 9in drums.

TYRES: Saloon/convertible 5.00, 5.25 or 5.60 x 15; estate 5.60 x 15.

SUSPENSION: Front independent coil springs and wishbones, rear semi-elliptic leaf springs, telescopic shock absorbers.

STEERING: Burman recirculating ball.

DIMENSIONS: Length: 13ft 7.5in (4153mm);

Steering column gear change layout.

width: 5ft 0.75in (1543mm); height: saloon
4ft 11.5in (1511mm), convertible 4ft 10in
(1473mm), estate 5ft 1in (1549mm);
weight: saloon 1 ton 0cwt 3qtr 6lb (1057kg),
convertible 1 ton 1cwt 0qtr 16lb (1074kg),
estate 1 ton 1cwt 3qtr 14lb (1111kg); turning
circle: 36ft (10.9m).
CAPACITIES: Fuel gallons (45 litres). Boot:
saloon/convertible 13.5ft³ (0.4m³), estate 26
or 44ft³ (0.8 or 1.32m³).

Singer Gazelle series 3a

Introduced in 1959, the series 3a was
mechanically similar to the series 3 it
replaced, it did, however, feature twin Solex
carburettors and revised gear ratios. The
rear of the car now featured rear fins and
separate light lenses of a style that would
be carried over until 1963, the windscreen
was enlarged, and headlamp cowls were now
the same colour as the main body. Standard
equipment included oil pressure gauge,
ammeter, windscreen washers, overriders,
and rim finishers. Optional extras: heater,
radio, clock, Laycock overdrive or Easidrive
automatic transmission, and more.

COLOURS (1959): Two-tone, main body
colour first, second is side flash and estate
roof. Saloon: Windsor blue/Foam white,
Fathom grey/Glacier blue, Burgundy/Ascot grey,
Embassy black/Windsor blue, Smoke green/

The car above was the first Rootes car owned by the author's brother: a Smoke green/Sage green Gazelle series 3a.

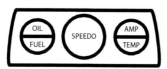

Instrument layout.

Sage green, Cloud rose/Foam white. Estate: Smoke green/Sage green, Windsor blue/ Foam white, Ascot grey/Burgundy, Charcoal/Windsor blue. Convertible: Powder blue/Moonstone with Powder blue hood, Pippin red/Pearl grey with Pippin red hood, Embassy black/Powder blue with black hood, Smoke green/Sage green with green hood, Pearl grey/Pippin red with Pippin red hood, all above available with black hood.

ENGINE: Four-cylinder OHV, bore 79mm, stroke 76.2mm, 1494cc, maximum bhp 64 at 4600rpm, twin Solex 32PBIS carburettors.

GEARBOX: Four-speed, floor-mounted gear change standard with steering column gear change, overdrive or automatic optional, synchromesh on top three gears. Ratios: saloon/convertible, top 4.55:1, 3rd 6.34:1, 2nd 9.75:1, 1st 15.24:1, reverse 19.31:1, with automatic, top 4.55, 2nd 7.243, 1st 13.497, reverse 14.014; estate, top 4.78:1, 3rd 6.65:1, 2nd 10.23:1, 1st 15.99:1, reverse 20.25:1.

REAR AXLE: Semi-floating, spiral bevel, ratio: saloon/convertible 4.55:1, manual or automatic, with overdrive 4.78:1, estate 4.78:1 with or without overdrive.

BRAKES: Lockheed, front and rear 9in drums.

TYRES: Saloon/convertible 5.60 x 15; estate 5.50 x 15 or 5.90 x 15.

SUSPENSION: Front independent coil springs and wishbones, rear semi-elliptic leaf springs, telescopic shock absorbers all round.

STEERING: Burman recirculating ball.

Left manual gear change layout; right automatic gear change layout.

DIMENSIONS: Length: 13ft 7.5in (4153mm); **width:** 5ft 0.75in (1543mm); **height:** saloon 4ft 11.5in (1511mm), convertible 4ft 10in (1473mm), estate 5ft 1in (1549mm); **weight:** saloon 1 ton 0cwt 3qtr 6lb (1057kg), convertible 1 ton 1cwt 0qtr 16lb (1074kg), estate 1 ton 1cwt 3qtr 14lb (1111kg); **turning circle:** 36ft (10.9m).
CAPACITIES: Fuel 10 gallons (45 litres). Boot: saloon/convertible 13.5ft^3 (0.4m^3), estate 26 or 44ft^3 (0.8 or 1.32m^3).

Singer Gazelle series 3b

Introduced in 1960, the series 3b had a hypoid bevel rear axle but reverted to a single carburettor. Appearance-wise, it was identical to the 3a, although there was a change to some of the colour schemes. Standard equipment included oil pressure gauge, ammeter, windscreen washers, overriders, rim finishers, and wood trimmed dashboard and doors. Optional extras: heater, radio, clock, individual front seats, Laycock overdrive or Easidrive automatic transmission, and more.

COLOURS (1960): Two-tone, main body colour first, second is side flash and estate roof. Saloon: Lake blue/Foam white, Fathom grey/Glacier blue, Burgundy/Cavalry beige,

Left: series 1, 2, 2a, 3; right: series 3a through to 6, showing the increased size of the later cars' windscreens.

Biarritz blue/Windsor blue, Smoke green/ Sage green. Single tones, Black, Biarritz blue. Estate: Smoke green/Sage green, Lake blue/Foam white, Charcoal/Windsor blue. Convertible: Powder blue/Moonstone with Powder blue hood, Pippin red/Moonstone with Pippin red hood, Moonstone/Morocco brown with Morocco brown hood, Smoke green/Sage green with green hood, Moonstone/Pippin red with Pippin red hood, all above available with black hood.

ENGINE: Four-cylinder OHV, bore 79mm, stroke 76.2mm, 1494cc, maximum bhp 64 at 4600rpm, Solex 32PBIS carburettor.

GEARBOX: Four-speed, floor-mounted gear change standard with steering column gear change, overdrive or automatic optional, synchromesh on top three gears. Ratios: saloon/convertible, top 4.44:1, 3rd 6.19:1, 2nd 9.51:1, 1st 14.87:1, reverse 18.84:1; saloon/convertible with overdrive and all estates with or without, o/d top 3.90, top 4.86, o/d 3rd 5.43, 3rd 6.76, 2nd 10.40, 1st 16.25, reverse 20.59.

REAR AXLE: Semi-floating, hypoid bevel, ratio: saloon/convertible 4.44:1, with overdrive

Instrument layout.

95

The car above has had original reflectors replaced by reversing lights, and then non-standard reflectors have been fitted to the rear bumper.

4.86:1; estate 4.86:1 with or without overdrive.
BRAKES: Lockheed, front and rear 9in drums.
TYRES: Saloon/convertible 5.60 x 15, estate 5.50 x 15 or 5.90 x 15.
SUSPENSION: Front independent coil springs and wishbones, rear semi-elliptic leaf springs, telescopic shock absorbers all round.
STEERING: Burman recirculating ball.
DIMENSIONS: Length: 13ft 7.5in (4153mm); **width:** 5ft 0.75in (1543mm); **height:** saloon 4ft 11.5in (1511mm), convertible 4ft 10in (1473mm), estate 5ft 1in (1549mm); **weight:** saloon 1 ton 0cwt 3qtr 6lb (1057kg), convertible 1 ton 1cwt 0qtr 16lb (1074kg), estate 1 ton 1cwt 3qtr 14lb (1111kg); **turning circle:** 36ft (10.9m).
CAPACITIES: Fuel 10 gallons (45 litres). Boot: saloon/convertible 13.5ft³ (0.4m³), estate 26 or 44ft³ (0.8 or 1.32m³).

Floor gear change layout.

Singer Gazelle series 3c

Introduced in 1961 to replace the series 3b, the series 3c featured an enlarged engine of 1592cc, the same as that used in the new Singer Vogue. Visually it was identical to the 3b with the exception of 1600 badging on the leading edge of the front doors, and was to be the last of the Gazelles with roll over style rear wings. Standard equipment as series 3b. Optional extras: heater (standard from 1962) radio, clock, Laycock overdrive or Easidrive automatic transmission, and more.

COLOURS (1961): Two-tone, main body colour first, second is side flash and estate roof. Saloon: Smoke green/Sage green, Lake blue/Foam white, Biarritz blue/Windsor blue, Fathom grey/Glacier blue, Burgundy/Cavalry beige, Foam white/Pippin red. Single tones, Black, Biarritz blue. Estate: Smoke green/Sage green, Charcoal/Windsor blue, Lake blue/Foam white. Convertible: Smoke green/Sage green with green hood, Pippin red/Moonstone with Pippin red hood. Moonstone/Pippin red with Pippin red hood, Powder blue/Moonstone with Powder blue hood, Moonstone/Morocco brown with Morocco brown hood, all above available with black hood.

ENGINE: Four-cylinder OHV, bore 81.5mm, stroke 76.2mm, 1592cc, maximum bhp 56.5 at 4100rpm, Zenith 30VN downdraught carburettor.

GEARBOX: Four-speed, floor-mounted gear change, overdrive or automatic optional, synchromesh on top three gears. Ratios:

Instrument layout.

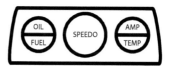

Left, below, is hubcap (nave plate) and rim finisher fitted as standard to series 3 to 3c cars. Right is wheel trim disc as found on series 5 and 6 cars, but occasionally seen on earlier cars.

saloon/convertible/estate, top 4.22:1, 3rd
5.88:1, 2nd 9.04:1, 1st 15.82:1, reverse
21.09:1, with automatic, top 4.22, 2nd 6.76,
1st 13.66, reverse 14.18, with overdrive, o/d
top 3.9, top 4.86, o/d 3rd 5.43, 3rd 7.76, 2nd
10.4, 1st 18.19, reverse 24.26.
REAR AXLE: Semi-floating, hypoid bevel,
ratio: 4.22:1 manual or automatic, 4.86:1 with
overdrive.
BRAKES: Lockheed, front and rear 9in drums.
TYRES: Saloon/convertible 5.60 x 15; estate
5.50 x 15 or 5.90 x 15.
SUSPENSION: Front independent coil springs
and wishbones, rear semi-elliptic leaf springs,
telescopic shock absorbers.
STEERING: Burman recirculating ball.

*Left manual gear change layout, right
automatic gear change layout.*

DIMENSIONS: Length: 13ft 7.5in (4153mm);
width: 5ft 0.75in (1543mm); **height:** saloon
4ft 11.5in (1511mm), convertible 4ft 10in
(1473mm), estate 5ft 1in (1549mm); **weight:**
saloon 1 ton 0cwt 3qtr 12lb (1060kg, dry
1019kg), convertible 1 ton 1cwt 0qtr 22lb
(1077kg, dry 1036kg), estate 1 ton 1cwt 2qtr
18lb (1100kg, dry 1060kg); **turning circle:**
36ft (10.9m).
CAPACITIES: Fuel 10 gallons (45 litres). Boot:
saloon/convertible 13.5ft^3 (0.4m^3), estate 26
or 44ft^3 (0.8 or 1.32m^3).

Singer Gazelle series 5

Introduced in 1963, the series 5 was an all-new body style to replace the series 3c. Also new were front disc brakes, the elimination of all greasing points, revised overriders with rubber inserts, and a completely different style of dashboard. An ammeter and oil pressure gauge were no longer fitted as standard, and optional automatic transmission was now Borg-Warner instead of Easidrive. An all synchromesh gearbox, fully reclining front seats and minor changes to colour schemes were introduced from late 1964. There was no series 4 – the vehicle initially designated as the series 4 was launched as the Vogue in 1961. The only model available was a saloon, the Gazelle 3c estate was discontinued in May 1962 and replaced by the Vogue estate, the Gazelle 3c convertible was discontinued in October 1962 and was not replaced by either a Gazelle or Vogue model. The rear wings reverted to a simpler style similar to the series 1 to 3 cars and the rear lights were now the same as those used on the Hillman Minx series 5. Standard equipment included heater, individual front seats, windscreen washers, front disc brakes, overriders, and wheel trim discs. Optional extras: radio, clock, oil pressure gauge, ammeter, Laycock overdrive or Borg-Warner automatic transmission, whitewall tyres, and more.

Instrument layout for series 5 and series 6 cars as below. Some gauges are optional.

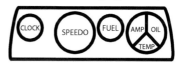

Note: separate heater slider controls for screen and car interior – hence you can have cold air to the face and warm air to the feet; a feature common to many Rootes cars during the 1960s.

COLOURS (1963): Two-tone, main body colour first, second is side flash. Smoke green/ Sage green, Lake blue/Foam white, Biarritz blue/Windsor blue, Dawn mist/Charcoal, Maroon/Cavalry beige, Foam white/Pippin red. Single tones, Embassy black, Biarritz blue, and metallics – Silver grey, Sapphire blue.
ENGINE: Four-cylinder OHV, bore 81.5mm, stroke 76.2mm, 1592cc, maximum bhp 56.5 at 4100rpm, Zenith 30VN carburettor.
GEARBOX: Four-speed, floor-mounted gear change, overdrive or automatic optional, synchromesh on top three gears. Ratios: top 3.89:1, 3rd 5.41:1, 2nd 8.32:1, 1st 14.57:1, reverse 19.42:1; with automatic, top 3.89, 2nd 5.64, 1st 9.31, reverse 8.14; with overdrive, o/d top 3.39, top 4.22, o/d 3rd 4.72, 3rd 5.88, 2nd 9.04, 1st 15.82, reverse 21.1.
REAR AXLE: Semi-floating, hypoid bevel, ratio 3.89:1 manual or automatic, 4.22 with overdrive.
BRAKES: Lockheed, front 10.3in discs, rear 9in drums.
TYRES: 6.00 x 13.
SUSPENSION: Front independent coil springs and wishbones, rear semi-elliptic leaf springs, telescopic shock absorbers.
STEERING: Burman recirculating ball.
DIMENSIONS: Length: 13ft 8.5in (4178mm); **width:** 5ft 0.75in (1543mm); **height:** 4ft 10in (1473mm); **weight:** 1 ton 0cwt 0qtr 12lb (1021kg); **turning circle:** 36ft (11m).
CAPACITIES: Fuel 10 gallons (45 litres). Boot 13.5ft³ (0.4m³).

Floor gear change layout.

Note: handbrake by the side of driver's seat; a usual feature of Rootes cars in the 1960s.

Singer Gazelle series 6

Introduced in 1965 to replace the series 5, the series 6 now had a 1725cc engine, and a revised front grille, making it appear even more like the Minx. This was the last of the series cars, as in 1966 the Arrow range would be introduced, initially as Hunter and Vogue saloons to replace the Hillman Super Minx and Singer Vogue, followed by Minx and Gazelles with smaller engines in 1967. Standard equipment included heater, individual reclining front seats, windscreen washers, front disc brakes, overriders, and wheel trims. Optional extras: radio, clock, oil pressure gauge, ammeter, seat belts, Laycock overdrive or Borg-Warner automatic transmission, whitewall tyres, and more.

COLOURS (1965): Two-tone, main body colour first, second is side flash. Dawn mist/ Charcoal, Holly green/Willow green, Maroon/ Cavalry beige, Foam white/Pippin red, Silver grey metallic/Embassy black, Royal blue

Rear wing trims as follows:
Top left series 1; middle series 2 and 2a; top right series 3;
bottom left series 3a, 3b, 3c; bottom right series 5 and 6.

Three different types of rear lights were used, dependent on the shape of the rear wings.

Interior of car with automatic transmission; for instrument layout see series 5 on previous pages.

101

metallic/Dawn mist, Silver Moss metallic/
Embassy black. Single tones, Embassy black,
and metallics – Royal blue, Lavender grey.
COLOURS (1966): Two-tone, main body
colour first, second is side flash. Polar white/
Embassy black, Polar white/Tartan red, Tartan
red/Embassy black, Midnight blue/Dawn mist,
Dawn mist/Midnight blue, Silver grey/Embassy
black. Single tones, Embassy black, Polar
white, Tartan red, Dawn mist, Holly green,
Midnight blue, Maroon.
ENGINE: Four-cylinder OHV, bore 81.5mm,
stroke 82.55mm, 1725cc, maximum bhp
69.5 at 4800rpm, Zenith 34IV downdraught
carburettor.
GEARBOX: Four-speed, floor-mounted gear
change, overdrive or automatic optional,
synchromesh on all forward gears. Ratios: top
3.89:1, 3rd 5.41:1, 2nd 8.32:1, 1st 13.04:1,
reverse 13.88:1.
REAR AXLE: Semi-floating, hypoid bevel, ratio
3.89:1.
BRAKES: Lockheed, front 10.3in discs, rear
9in drums.
TYRES: 6.00 x 13.
SUSPENSION: Front independent coil springs
and wishbones, rear semi-elliptic leaf springs
and telescopic shock absorbers.
STEERING: Burman recirculating ball.
DIMENSIONS: Length: 13ft 8.5in (4178mm);
width: 5ft 0.75in (1543mm); **height:** 4ft 10in
(1473mm); **weight:** 1 ton 0cwt 0qtr 10lb
(1020kg, dry 979kg); **turning circle:** 36 ft
(10.9 m).
CAPACITIES: Fuel 10 gallons (45 litres). Boot
13.5ft^3 (0.4m^3).

Floor gear change layouts, manual on left and automatic on right.

The car above is fitted with an external screen visor, something occasionally found on cars of the 1960s.

Singer Vogue mark 1

Introduced in 1961, the second Rootes Singer, the Vogue mark 1 was originally conceived as a replacement for the Gazelle, but instead became a model in its own right. Available initially as a saloon and from February 1962 as an estate. The saloon can be easily distinguished from the mark 2 model by its cylindrical boot lock and its overriders without rubber inserts. It also had white front indicator lenses initially, however these were subsequently changed. The 1961 retail price was £956, a Gazelle was £840 and a Super Minx £854. Standard equipment included heater, oil pressure gauge, ammeter, and screen washers. Optional extras: radio, Laycock overdrive or Easidrive automatic transmission, reversing lights, and more.

The blue and white car above appears to have the same rear lights as those fitted on the Gazelle models; the blue car below right and estate cars on the next page are fitted with the earlier all white front indicators and sidelights, whilst the blue and white cars above and maroon cars below have the later amber front indicators.

COLOURS (1961): Two-tone, main body colour first, second is roof. Lake blue/Foam white, Biarritz blue/Windsor blue, Smoke green/Sage green, Foam white/Pippin red, Fathom grey/ Glazier blue, Burgundy/Cavalry beige. Single tones, Lake blue, Biarritz blue, Smoke green, Foam white, Fathom grey, Burgundy, Embassy black.
ENGINE: Four-cylinder OHV, bore 81.5mm, stroke 76.2mm, 1592cc, maximum bhp 66.25 at 4800rpm, Solex 32PBIS2 carburettor.
GEARBOX: Four-speed, floor-mounted gear change, overdrive or automatic optional,

Left is hub cap (nave plate) and rim finisher, fitted to early Vogues. Right is wheel trim disc, fitted to later cars.

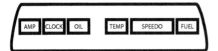

Instrument layout. Note: indicator stalk is on right of steering column; as was usual for most British cars during the 1960s.

synchromesh on top three gears. Ratios: top 4.22:1, 3rd 5.88:1, 2nd 9.04:1, 1st 14.13:1, reverse 17.89:1; with overdrive, o/d top 3.57, top 4.44, o/d 3rd 4.97, 3rd 6.93, 2nd 9.51, 1st 14.87, reverse 18.84; with automatic, top 4.22, 2nd 6.75, 1st 13.67, reverse 14.18.
REAR AXLE: Semi-floating, hypoid bevel, ratio manual or automatic 4.22:1, with overdrive 4.44:1.
BRAKES: Lockheed, front and rear 9in drums.
TYRES: 5.90 x 13.
SUSPENSION: Front independent coil springs and semi-trailing wishbones, rear semi-elliptic leaf springs, telescopic shock absorbers.
STEERING: Burman recirculating ball.
DIMENSIONS: Length: 13ft 9.25in (4197mm); **width:** 5ft 2.25in (1581mm); **height:** 4ft 10.25in (1480mm); **weight:** saloon 1 ton 1cwt 3qtr 19lb (1114kg, dry 1069kg); **turning circle:** 36ft (11m).

CAPACITIES: Fuel 11 gallons (49 litres). Boot: saloon 14.5ft^3 (0.4m^3), estate 28.5 or 46ft^3 (0.8 or 1.4m^3).

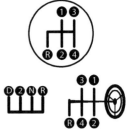

Above: Top is standard floor gear change layout; bottom left is optional automatic; bottom right is optional steering column gear change.

Singer Vogue mark 2

Introduced in 1962 to replace the mark 1, the mark 2 now featured front disc brakes, separate front seats and elimination of all greasing points. In addition, repositioning the fuel tank increased boot space by 1.5ft³, and a Borg-Warner automatic gearbox replaced the Smiths Easidrive. Unlike its Hillman Super Minx mark 2 counterpart, however, there was no convertible version. Standard equipment included heater with two-speed fan, oil pressure gauge, ammeter, two-speed wipers, screen washers, reversing lights, overriders, and wheel trim discs. Optional extras: radio, clock, seat belts, Laycock overdrive or Borg-Warner automatic transmission, and more.

Instrument layout.

This car below has been fitted with side repeater indicators – something that many later owners did to '60s cars, and that is now standard equipment on most modern cars. It has also been fitted with mark 1 type overriders without rubber inserts; there are no overriders on the back bumper.

COLOURS (1963): Two-tone, main body colour first, second is roof. Saloon: Dawn mist/Charcoal, Biarritz blue/Windsor blue, Velvet green/Sage green, Foam white/Pippin red, Maroon/Cavalry beige. Single tones, Biarritz blue, Velvet green, Foam white, Maroon, Dawn mist, Embassy black, and metallics – Silver Moss, Silver grey, Lavender grey, Burnt almond. Estate: Dawn mist/Charcoal, Lake blue/Foam white, Smoke green/Sage green, Charcoal/Windsor blue. Single tones, Lake blue, Smoke green, Charcoal, Dawn mist.
ENGINE: Four-cylinder OHV, bore 81.5mm, stroke 76.2mm, 1592cc, maximum bhp 62 at 4400rpm, Solex 33PSEI carburettor.

GEARBOX: Four-speed, floor-mounted gear change overdrive or automatic optional, synchromesh on top three gears, ratios saloon only, top 3.89:1, 3rd 5.41:1, 2nd 8.32:1, 1st 13.01:1, reverse 16.48:1, saloon with overdrive and estates with or without, o/d top 3.39, top 4.22, o/d 3rd 4.72, 3rd 5.87, 2nd 9.04, 1st 14.13, reverse 17.89.
REAR AXLE: Semi-floating, hypoid bevel, ratio: saloon 3.89:1, saloon with overdrive 4.22:1, estate with or without overdrive 4.22:1.
BRAKES: Lockheed, front 10.3in discs, rear 9in drums.
TYRES: 6.00 x 13.
SUSPENSION: Front independent coil springs and semi-trailing wishbones, rear semi-elliptic leaf springs, telescopic shock absorbers.
STEERING: Burman recirculating ball.

Left is standard floor gear change layout; right is optional steering column automatic gear change layout.

DIMENSIONS: Length: 13ft 9.25in (4197mm); **width:** 5ft 2.25in (1581mm); **height:** 4ft 10.25in (1480mm); **weight:** saloon 1 ton 1cwt 1qtr 24lb (1090kg), estate 1 ton 2cwt 2qtr 13lb (1126kg); **turning circle:** 36ft (11m).
CAPACITIES: Fuel: saloon 10.5 gallons (48 litres), estate 10 gallons (45 litres). Boot: saloon 16ft³ (0.5m³), estate 28.5 or 46ft³ (0.8 or 1.4m³).

Singer Vogue mark 3

Introduced in 1964, the mark 3 featured a new squarer look – the result of changes to the front and rear glass area. The estate received the new more upright front windscreen, but the rear remained unchanged. The Vogue now had synchromesh on all forward gears, fully reclining front seats, and an increase in engine power, the result of fitting the aluminium cylinder head as used in the Humber Sceptre and Sunbeam Rapier. The estate now had overriders with rubber inserts. Standard equipment included heater, fully reclining front seats, two-speed wipers, screen washers, twin reversing lights, overriders, and wheel trim discs. Optional extras: radio, clock, seat belts, Laycock overdrive or Borg-Warner automatic transmission, wing mirrors, and more.

COLOURS (1964): Saloon: single tones only, Biarritz blue, Velvet green, Foam white, Maroon, Dawn Mist, Embassy black, and metallics – Silver grey, Lavender grey, Silver moss, Burnt almond. Estate: two-tone, main body colour first, second is roof. Biarritz blue/Dawn mist, Velvet green/Sage green, Silver moss metallic/Embassy black, Single tones, Biarritz blue, Velvet green, and metallics – Silver grey, Silver moss, Burnt almond.

The car on the left has been fitted with a vinyl roof; this was not a Vogue option, so presumably was a customised item made for this particular car.

Instrument layout.

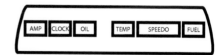

ENGINE: Four-cylinder OHV, bore 81.5mm, stroke 76.2mm, 1592cc, maximum bhp 78.5 at 5000rpm, Solex 32PAIA twin choke carburettor.

GEARBOX: Four-speed, floor-mounted gear change, overdrive or automatic optional, synchromesh on all forward gears. Ratios: saloon, top 3.89:1, 3rd 5.41:1, 2nd 8.32:1, 1st 13.04:1, reverse 13.88:1; with automatic, top 4.22, 2nd 6.12, 1st 10.1, reverse 8.84; estate, top 4.22:1, 3rd 5.871:1, 2nd 9.04:1, 1st 14.16:1, reverse 15.07:1.

REAR AXLE: Semi-floating, hypoid bevel, ratio saloon 3.89:1, saloon with overdrive or automatic options 4.22:1, estate with or without overdrive or automatic 4.22:1.

BRAKES: Lockheed, front 10.3in discs, rear 9in drums.

TYRES: 6.00 x 13 saloon, 6.50 x 13 estate.

SUSPENSION: Front independent coil springs and wishbones, rear semi-elliptic leaf springs, telescopic shock absorbers.

STEERING: Burman recirculating ball.

Left is standard floor gear change layout, right is optional steering column automatic gear change layout.

DIMENSIONS: Length: 13ft 11in (4242mm); **width:** 5ft 3in (1600mm); **height:** 4ft 10in (1473mm); **weight:** saloon 1 ton 1cwt 0qtr 19lb (1075kg), estate 1 ton 2cwt 0qtr 24lb (1128kg); **turning circle:** 36ft (11m).

CAPACITIES: Fuel saloon 10.5 gallons (48 litres), estate 10 gallons (45 litres). Boot: saloon 16ft³ (0.5m³), estate 28.5 or 44ft³ (0.8 or 1.4m³).

Rear lights as used for saloon and estate models: left: Hillman Super Minx; right: Singer Vogue (pre-Arrow range).

Singer Vogue mark 4

Introduced in 1965, the mark 4 would be the last of the current Vogue range, with the new Arrow range of Rootes vehicles appearing during October 1966. The mark 4 estate, however, would continue until April 1967, as the new Arrow Vogue was only initially available as a saloon. New for the mark 4 version was a 1725cc engine, as featured in the Gazelle series 6, an alternator instead of a dynamo and silver headlight surrounds. Standard equipment included heater, oil pressure gauge, ammeter, fully reclining front seats, screen washers, twin reversing lights, overriders, and wheel trim discs. Optional extras: radio, seat belts, Laycock overdrive or Borg-Warner automatic transmission, fog and spotlights, and more.

COLOURS (1965): Saloon: Holly green, Foam white, Maroon, Dawn mist, Embassy black, and metallics – Royal blue, Silver moss, Silver grey, Lavender grey, Burnt almond. Estate: Two-tone, main body colour first, second is roof. Holly green/Willow green, Royal blue metallic/Dawn mist, Silver moss metallic/ Embassy black. Single tones, Holly green, and metallics – Royal blue, Silver grey, Silver moss, Burnt almond.
COLOURS (1966): Estate: single tones only, Holly green, and metallics – Shadow blue, Silver grey, Silver moss, Burnt almond.
ENGINE: Four-cylinder OHV, bore 81.5mm, stroke 82.55mm, 1725cc, maximum bhp 91 at 5500rpm, Solex PAIAS twin choke carburettor.
GEARBOX: Four-speed, floor-mounted gear

Instrument layout.

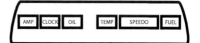

change, overdrive or automatic optional,
synchromesh on all forward gears. Ratios:
saloon top 3.89:1, 3rd 5.41:1, 2nd 8.32:1,
1st 13.04:1, reverse 13.88:1, saloon with
overdrive and estate with or without, o/d
top 3.38:1, top 4.22:1, o/d 3rd 4.73:1, 3rd
5.88:1, 2nd 9.04:1, 1st 14.16:1, reverse
15.07:1.
REAR AXLE: Semi-floating, hypoid bevel, ratio
saloon 3.89:1, saloon with overdrive 4.22;1,
estate with or without overdrive 4.22:1.
BRAKES: Lockheed, front 10.3in discs, rear
9in drums.
TYRES: 6.00 x 13 saloon, 6.50 x 13 estate.

*Car on the right has been fitted with
non-standard wheels.*

Floor gear change layout.

SUSPENSION: Front independent coil springs
and wishbones, rear semi-elliptic leaf springs,
telescopic shock absorbers.
STEERING: Burman recirculating ball.
DIMENSIONS: Length: 13ft 11in (4242mm);
width: 5ft 3in (1600mm); **height:** 4ft 10in
(1473mm); **weight:** saloon 1 ton 1cwt 0qtr
19lb (1075kg), estate 1 ton 2cwt 0qtr 24lb
(1128kg); **turning circle:** 36ft (11m).
CAPACITIES: Fuel: saloon 10.5 gallons (48
litres), estate 10 gallons (45 litres). Boot:
saloon 16ft^3 (0.5m^3), estate 28.5 or 46ft^3 (0.8
or 1.4m^3).

Singer Vogue

Introduced in 1966 to replace the Vogue mark 4, this was the first of the Arrow Singers to appear, initially only available as a saloon, the estate followed in 1967. The Hillman Hunter and the new Vogue were the first of the Rootes cars to feature MacPherson strut front suspension. This was almost the end of the Singer marque differences between it and the Hillmans now consisted of a vaguely different front grille and rectangular instead of circular headlights and from the rear the only difference was the Singer badge, it was discontinued in April 1970 and replaced by the Hunter GL. Standard equipment for 1967 included heater and ventilation system with blower, cigarette lighter, reclining front seats, coat hooks, reversing lights, overriders, and wheel trim discs. Optional extras: radio, Borg-Warner automatic transmission, fog and spotlights, wing mirrors, and more. Note: a 1969 Rootes optional accessories brochure includes items that are standard on today's cars. Items such as seat belts, head rests, interior bonnet release, exterior mirrors, and a rear window anti-condensation panel was available, instead of a heated rear screen.

For some overseas markets and also for a brief period at the end of Singer production in 1970, the Vogue was badged as a Sunbeam.

The stick-on rear screen heater/demister: a popular accessory before rear screen heaters became standard.

Instrument layout.

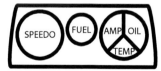

COLOURS (1966): Embassy black, Maroon, Polar white, and metallics – Silver grey, Sherwood green, Shadow blue, Burnt almond.

COLOURS (1967): Polar white, and metallics – Claret, Sherwood green, Midnight blue, Gunmetal, Golden sand.

ENGINE: Four-cylinder OHV, bore 81.5mm, stroke 82.5mm, 1725cc, maximum bhp 80 at 5000rpm, Stromberg 150CDS variable choke carburettor.

GEARBOX: Four-speed, floor-mounted gear change, synchromesh on all forward gears. Ratios: top 3.7:1, 3rd 5.15:1, 2nd 7.92:1, 1st 12.41:1, reverse 13.2:1, with automatic transmission, top 3.7, 2nd 5.365, 1st 8.843, reverse 7.733.

REAR AXLE: Semi-floating, hypoid bevel, ratio 3.7:1 manual or automatic.

BRAKES: Lockheed, front 9.6in discs, rear 9in drums.

TYRES: 5.60 x 13.
SUSPENSION: Fully independent MacPherson struts, coil springs and dampers, rear semi-elliptic leaf springs and telescopic dampers.
STEERING: Burman recirculating ball.

Floor gear change layouts, manual on left and optional automatic on right.

DIMENSIONS: Length: 14ft 1.5in (4305mm); **width:** 5ft 3.5in (1613mm); **height:** 4ft 8in (1422mm); **weight:** saloon 18cwt 2qtr 11lb (944kg); **turning circle:** 33ft 6in (10.2m).
CAPACITIES: Fuel 10 gallons (45 litres). Boot: saloon 18ft^3 (0.54m^3), estate 34 or 62ft^3 (1.0 or 1.8m^3).

A Singer Gazelle produced from 1967 to 1970, identical in appearance to the Singer Vogue, it had a smaller engine as detailed below, and was less well equipped, it was only available as a saloon.

ENGINE: Four-cylinder OHV, bore 81.5mm, stroke 71.6mm, 1496cc, maximum bhp 64 at 4800rpm, Zenith 150 CDS sidedraught carburettor.
GEARBOX: Four-speed, floor-mounted gear change, Borg Warner automatic transmission optional with 1725cc engine, synchromesh on all forward gears. Ratios: top 3.89:1, 3rd 5.41:1, 2nd 8.32:1, 1st 13.04:1, reverse 13.88:1
REAR AXLE: Semi-floating, hypoid bevel, ratio 3.89:1.

Singer Chamois

Introduced in 1964, the Chamois was followed by the mark 2 in 1965, the Chamois Sport in 1966 and Chamois Coupé in 1967. All versions featured single headlamps at first, but ended up with double headlamps. Sport models feature a red side strip, and ventilated engine cover, but other cars may have retrospectively been fitted with these. Interestingly, the Chamois featured wider wheels than the Hillman Imp, and the Sport was mechanically identical to the Sunbeam Imp Sport. All Chamois models were discontinued in March 1970. 1967 retail prices were as follows: Chamois £619, Chamois Coupé £665, seat belt £3 5s (£3.25), reversing light £2 17s 6d (£2.75). Standard equipment for 1965 included heater with blower, screen washers, overriders, and wheel trim discs. Optional extras: radio, seat belts, reversing lights, and more.

COLOURS (1964): Main body colour first, second is side flash. Embassy black/Foam white, Balmoral grey/Embassy black, Forest green/Foam white, Maroon/Foam white, Loch blue/Foam white, Foam white/Tartan red.
ENGINE: Four-cylinder OHV (rear-mounted), bore 68mm, stroke 60.37mm, 875cc,

maximum bhp 42 at 5000rpm, Solex 30PIHT (auto choke) or Solex 30PIH5 carburettor.
GEARBOX/REAR AXLE: Four-speed, synchromesh on all forward gears, combined gearbox and hypoid bevel transaxle. Ratios: top 4.138:1, 3rd 5.702:1, 2nd 8.905:1, 1st 16.595:1, reverse 13.824:1, final drive 4.857:1.
BRAKES: Front and rear 8in drums.
TYRES: 5.50 x 12.
SUSPENSION: Front independent coil/swing axle, rear independent coil/trailing links.
STEERING: Rack and pinion.
DIMENSIONS: Length: 11ft 9.25in (3588mm); **width:** 5ft 0.75in (1543mm); **height:** 4ft 6.5in (1384mm); **weight:** 14cwt 0qtr 25lb (722kg); **turning circle:** 30ft 6in (9.3m).
CAPACITIES: Fuel 6 gallon (27 litres). Boot front 3.25ft³, rear 5ft³ or 16.5ft³ with rear seat lowered (combined 0.25m³ or 0.6m³).

Previous page and above are mark 1 models.

Floor gear change layout, all models.

Above: mark 2 models; below: face-lifted models from 1968 onwards.

Some cars on these pages have non-standard wheels; usual wheel and trim is shown on right.

Instrument layout.

Singer Chamois Sport

Specification for Singer Chamois Sport as Singer Chamois except as follows:
Standard equipment included reclining front seats and an oil cooler.

ENGINE: Maximum bhp 55 at 6100rpm, twin Stromberg 125CD carburettors.

BRAKES: Power assisted 8in front and rear drums.

WEIGHT: 14cwt 2qtr 20lb (745kg).

COLOURS (1965 to 1967): Main body colour first, second is side flash, Forest green/Polar white, Oxford blue/Polar white, Coffee brown/Polar white, Embassy black/Polar white (1965 only), Polar white/Tartan red (1965 only), Polar white/Oxford blue (1966/1967 – replaces Polar white/Tartan red), Maroon/Polar white (1965/1966), Claret metallic/Polar white (1967 replaces Maroon).

Above: Chamois Coupé as introduced in 1967; below: face-lifted Chamois Coupé from 1968 onwards. All Chamois models had overriders as standard until the introduction of twin headlight models.

Sunbeam-Talbot 90

Introduced in 1948 the Sunbeam-Talbot 90 was the first true post-war car. Also available was the Sunbeam-Talbot 80, which used a smaller Minx derived engine. These early cars are rarely seen at car shows, the saloon on the right (top two pictures) is a 90 model and is missing its rear wheel spats, the saloon below and the convertible are 80 models, and it should also be noted that all cars shown on this page and some of those on the following pages are fitted with non-standard amber indicators, and that the two-tone colour scheme was introduced with the mark 3.

COLOURS: Black, Gun, Ruby, Silver green, Satin bronze.
ENGINE: 80 – Four-cylinder OHV, bore 63mm, stroke 95mm, 1185cc, maximum bhp 47 at 4800rpm, Stromberg DBA36 carburettor. 90 – Four-cylinder OHV, bore 75mm, stroke 110mm, 1944cc, maximum bhp 64 at 4100rpm, Stromberg DBA36 carburettor.
GEARBOX: Four-speed, steering column gear change. Synchromesh on top three gears.
REAR AXLE: Spiral bevel 5.22:1 (80), 4.31:1 (90).
BRAKES: Lockheed, front and rear 10in drums, (80 model with 9in drums).
TYRES: 5.50 x 16in.
SUSPENSION: Front beam axle, semi-elliptic leaf springs, rear semi-elliptic leaf springs.
STEERING: Burman worm and nut.
DIMENSIONS: Length: 13ft 11.5in (4254mm); **width:** 5ft 2in (1575mm); **height:** 5ft 0.75in (1543mm); **weight:** 1 ton 5cwt 1qtr 2lb (1233kg).

Sunbeam-Talbot 90 mark 2

The mark 2 was introduced in 1950, with a new chassis frame incorporating coil and wishbone independent front suspension. The front end was revised with raised headlights, and the fog/driving lights were replaced with additional air vents. An enlarged engine was also fitted, and the 80 model was dropped. Standard equipment included map reading light, reversing lights, rear wheel spats, and comprehensive tool kit. Optional extras: heater, radio, overriders, and more.

COLOURS (1950): Black, Satin bronze, Gun, Beech green, Light metallic blue.
ENGINE: Four-cylinder OHV, bore 81mm, stroke 110mm, 2267cc, maximum bhp 70 at 4000rpm, Stromberg DBA36 carburettor.
GEARBOX: Four-speed, steering column gear change, synchromesh on top three gears. Ratios: top 3.9:1, 3rd 5.81:1, 2nd 9.63:1, 1st 12.43:1, reverse 15.74:1.
REAR AXLE: Hypoid bevel, ratio 3.9:1.
BRAKES: Lockheed, front and rear 10in drums.
TYRES: 5.50 x 16.
SUSPENSION: Front independent with coil springs and wishbones, rear semi-elliptic leaf springs.
STEERING: Burman recirculating ball.
DIMENSIONS: Length: 13ft 11.5in (4254mm); **width:** 5ft 2.5in (1587mm); **height:** 4ft 8in (1422mm); **weight:** 1 ton 5cwt 1qtr 21lb (1318kg); **turning circle:** 36ft (11m).
CAPACITIES: Fuel 10 gallons (45 litres).

Steering column gear change layout.

Instrument layout.

Sunbeam-Talbot mark 2a

The mark 2a was introduced in 1952, with more powerful engine and larger 10in brakes; the rear spats were deleted, and perforated wheels fitted to aid brake cooling. This would be the last vehicle to carry the Talbot name until the takeover by Peugeot. It was a very successful rally car, winning prizes in the Monte Carlo, French Alpine, Austrian Alpine, Lisbon and RAC rallies, in the hands of Stirling Moss, George Hartwell, Sheila Van Damm, and other famous drivers. Standard equipment included reversing lights and rim finishers. Optional extras included heater/ventilator, radio, and overriders.

COLOURS (1952): Black, Gun, Sapphire blue, Beech green, Alpine mist, Satin bronze.
ENGINE: Four-cylinder OHV, bore 81mm, stroke 110mm, 2267cc, maximum bhp 77 at 4100rpm, Stromberg DBA36 carburettor.
GEARBOX: Four-speed, steering column gear change, synchromesh on top three gears. Ratios: top 3.9:1, 3rd 5.81:1, 2nd 9.63:1, 1st 12.43:1, reverse 15.74:1.
REAR AXLE: Hypoid bevel, ratio 3.9:1.
BRAKES: Lockheed, front and rear 10in drums.
TYRES: 5.50 x 16.
SUSPENSION: Front independent with coil springs and wishbones, rear semi-elliptic leaf springs.
STEERING: Burman recirculating ball.
DIMENSIONS: Length: 13ft 11.5in (4254mm); **width:** 5ft 2.5in (1587mm); **height:** 4ft 8in (1422mm); **weight:** 1 ton 6cwt 1qtr 10lb (1338kg); **turning circle:** 36ft (11m).
CAPACITIES: Fuel 10 gallons (45 litres).

Note: position of trafficator/indicator switch on top of steering cowl (as in photograph above) is typical of 1950s cars.

Sunbeam mark 3

The Sunbeam mark 3 was introduced in 1954, with new front end styling, chromed vents on sides in place of name plate, and reversing lights incorporated in rear number plate unit instead of rear lights, which now had a red lens. It was discontinued in 1957. Standard equipment included two-speed wipers, reversing lights, wheel trims with rim finishers, and comprehensive tool kit. Optional extras: heater/ventilator, radio, revolution counter, overdrive, overriders, whitewall tyres, and more.

The car above successfully completed the 1956 Monte Carlo Rally.

COLOURS (1956): Two-tone, lower body colour first, Pine green/Cactus green, Corinth blue/Dawn mist, Claret/Dove grey. Single tones, Embassy black, Claret, Thistle grey.
ENGINE: Four-cylinder OHV, bore 81mm stroke 110mm, 2267cc, maximum bhp 85 at 4400rpm, Zenith D136 carburettor.
GEARBOX: Four-speed, steering column gear change, overdrive optional, synchromesh on top three gears. Ratios: top 3.9:1, 3rd 5.81:1, 2nd 9.63:1, 1st 12.43:1, reverse 15.74:1.
REAR AXLE: Hypoid bevel, ratio 3.9:1.
BRAKES: Lockheed, front and rear 10in drums.
TYRES: 5.50 x 16.
SUSPENSION: Front independent coil, rear semi-elliptic leaf springs.
STEERING: Burman recirculating ball.
DIMENSIONS: Length: 13ft 11.5in (4254mm); **width:** 5ft 2.5in (1587mm); **height:** 4ft 8in (1422mm); **weight:** 1 ton 6cwt 1qtr 10lb (1338kg); **turning circle:** 36ft (11m).
CAPACITIES: Fuel 10 gallons (45 litres).

The two-tone paint scheme sometimes seen on earlier cars was in fact only introduced with the mark 3.

Steering column gear change layout.

Instrument layout.

119

Sunbeam Rapier series 1

Introduced during 1955, the first of the Audax range of cars was considered by some as having taken styling cues from the Hillman Californian. Standard equipment included oil pressure gauge, ammeter, fuel and water temperature gauges, cigarette lighter, two-speed wipers, Laycock overdrive, opening front quarter lights and wind-down rear quarter lights, and full wheel trims with rim finishers. Optional extras: heater, radio, clock, revolution counter, screen washers, reversing light, fog and spotlights, exterior mirrors, overriders, whitewall tyres, and more.

The Sunbeam Rapier was an extremely successful competition car, with over 40 class or outright wins in rallies and touring car races from 1956 to 1963, including Monte Carlo, RAC, Scottish, Silverstone, and Brands Hatch.

COLOURS (1956): Two-tone, lower body colour first, Pippin red/Pearl grey, Pearl grey/Summer blue, Honey beige/Pearl grey, Pearl grey/April yellow, Embassy black/April yellow, Embassy black/Mayfair grey, Dawn mist/Corinth blue.
ENGINE: Four-cylinder OHV, bore 76.2mm stroke 76.2mm, 1390cc maximum bhp 62.5 at 5000rpm with Stromberg DIF36 carburettor.

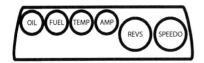

Instrument layout diagram above as per brochure and handbook, but note the photograph below of a series 1. Rapier dashboard has gauges arranged as series 2 cars.

(from Oct 1956: 67 bhp at 5400rpm with twin Zenith 36WIP2 carburettors).

GEARBOX: Four-speed, steering column gear change with overdrive, synchromesh on top three gears. Ratios: o/d top 3.95:1, top 5.22:1, o/d 3rd 5.89:1, 3rd 7.788:1, 2nd 12.905:1, 1st 16.642:1, reverse 21.08:1.

REAR AXLE: Semi-floating with spiral bevel, ratio 5.22:1.

BRAKES: Lockheed, front and rear 9in drums

TYRES: 5.60 x 15.

SUSPENSION: Front independent coil spring, rear semi-elliptic leaf springs, telescopic shock absorbers all round.

STEERING: Burman worm and nut.

DIMENSIONS: Length: 13ft 4.5in (4077mm); **width:** 5ft 0.75in (1543mm); **height:** 4ft 10.5in (1486mm); wheelbase 8ft 0in (2438mm); **weight:** 1 ton 0cwt 3qtr 26lb (1066kg); **turning circle:** 34ft 3in (10.5m).

CAPACITIES: Fuel 7.25 gallons (33 litres), from 1957 on 10 gallons (45 litres). Boot 13.5ft³ (0.4m³).

Steering column gear change layout.

121

Sunbeam Rapier series 2

Introduced in 1958 with tail fins that would remain a feature of the Rapier long after the Minx and Gazelle had lost theirs in 1963, the Rapier was now available as a convertible, and gained an enlarged engine of 1494cc, floor-mounted gear change, and revised steering, but overdrive was now an optional extra. 1958 retail prices: saloon £1108, and convertible £1164. (A Singer Gazelle saloon was £898 and a convertible was £999.) Standard equipment included oil pressure gauge, ammeter, fuel and water temperature gauges, cigarette lighter, two-speed wipers, opening front quarter lights and wind down rear quarter lights, and full wheel trims with rim finishers. Optional extras: heater, radio, clock, Laycock overdrive, reversing light, fog and spotlights, overriders, whitewall tyres, and more.

COLOURS (1958): Saloon/convertible: two-tone, main body colour first, second is side flash and saloon roof, Pearl grey/Pippin red with Pippin red hood, Cypress green/Iceberg green with Cypress green hood, Windsor blue/Corinth blue with Corinth blue hood, Corinth blue/Embassy black with black hood, Glacier blue/Embassy black with black hood, Moonstone/Morocco brown with Morocco brown hood, Morocco brown/Moonstone with Morocco brown hood. All convertibles available with black hood.
ENGINE: Four-cylinder OHV, bore 79mm, stroke 76.2mm, 1494cc, maximum bhp 73 at 5200rpm, twin Zenith 36WIP2 downdraught carburettors.

Instrument layout.

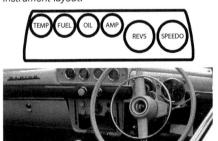

122

Left series 2, right series 3 onwards showing increased size of later car windscreens.

GEARBOX: Four-speed, floor-mounted gear change, overdrive optional, synchromesh on top three gears. Ratios: top 4.55:1, 3rd 6.794:1, 2nd 11.258:1, 1st 14.518:1, reverse 18.389:1, with overdrive, o/d top 3.612, top 4.78, o/d 3rd 5.387, 3rd 7.126, 2nd 11.807, 1st 15.227, reverse 19.288.

REAR AXLE: Semi-floating spiral bevel, ratio 4.55:1, with overdrive 4.78:1.

BRAKES: Lockheed, front 10in drums, rear 9in drums.

TYRES: 5.60 x 15.

SUSPENSION: Front independent coil, rear semi-elliptic leaf springs, telescopic shock absorbers all round.

STEERING: Burman recirculating ball.

DIMENSIONS: Length: 13ft 6.5in (4128mm); **width:** 5ft 0.75in (1543mm); **height:** saloon 4ft 10in (1473mm), convertible 4ft 9.5in (1460mm); **weight:** saloon 1 ton 1cwt 0qtr 18lb (1075kg), convertible 1 ton 1cwt 0qtr 14lb (1073kg); **turning circle:** 34ft 3in (10.5m).

CAPACITIES: Fuel 10 gallons (45 litres). Boot 13.5ft^3 (0.4m^3).

Floor gear change layout.

Sunbeam Rapier series 3

Introduced in 1959, and distinguished from the series 2 by its narrower side flash, the series 3 featured an aluminium cylinder head, front disc brakes, and a revised dashboard with wood veneer. The rear axle was changed from spiral bevel to hypoid a year after launch, but, unlike the Hillman Minx and Singer Gazelle, this did not result in a change to the series numbering. Standard equipment in addition to the series 2: front disc brakes. Optional extras: heater, radio, clock, revolution counter, Laycock overdrive, reversing light, overriders, and more.

Car on right was the 'founding car' of the Sunbeam Rapier Owners' club (SROC).

COLOURS (1959): Saloon/convertible: two-tone, main body colour first, second is side flash and saloon roof, Pearl grey/Pippin red with Pippin red hood, Ash grey/Pippin red with Pippin red hood, Velvet green/Sage green with Sage green hood, Moonstone/Powder blue with Powder blue hood, Powder blue/Corinth blue with Corinth blue hood, Moonstone/Morocco brown with Morocco brown hood. All convertibles available with black hood.
ENGINE: Four-cylinder OHV, bore 79mm, stroke 76.2mm, 1494cc, maximum bhp 78 at 5400rpm, twin Zenith 36WIA downdraught carburettors.
GEARBOX (1959): Four-speed, floor-mounted

Instrument layout. Note: indicator stalk is on right, as was usual for most 1960s British cars; overdrive switch is on left of steering column.

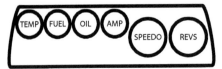

gear change, overdrive optional, synchromesh on top three gears. Ratios at launch: (later cars as 3a model) top 4.55:1, 3rd 6.341:1, 2nd 9.751:1, 1st 15.244:1, reverse 19.309:1; with overdrive, o/d top 3.84, top 4.78, o/d 3rd 5.34, 3rd 6.65, 2nd 10.23, 1st 15.99, reverse 20.25.
REAR AXLE: Semi-floating, spiral-bevel, ratio 4.55:1, with overdrive 4.78:1.
BRAKES: Lockheed, front 10.81in discs, rear 9in drums.
TYRES: 5.60 x 15.
SUSPENSION: Front independent coil, rear semi-elliptic leaf springs, telescopic shock absorbers all round.
STEERING: Burman recirculating ball.

Floor gear change layout.

DIMENSIONS: Length: 13ft 6.5in (4128mm); **width:** 5ft 0.75in (1543mm); **height:** saloon 4ft 10in (1473mm), convertible 4ft 9.5in (1460mm); **weight:** saloon 1 ton 1cwt 0qtr 8lb (1070kg), convertible 5lb less (1068kg); **turning circle:** 36ft (11m).
CAPACITIES: Fuel 10 gallons (45 litres). Boot 13.5ft^3 (0.4m^3).

Rear number plate arrangement:

Top – series 2.

Middle – series 3 and 3a.

Bottom – series 4 and 5.

Sunbeam Rapier series 3a

The 3a was introduced in 1961. Visually the same as the series 3 from the outside, the top half of the door trim was changed to a plain rather than quilted finish. It gained a 1592cc engine and was now available with single tone metallic paint finish, and a heater and screen washers were now fitted as standard. It was the last of the Rapiers to be available as a convertible. Standard equipment now included heater, ammeter, fuel and water temperature gauges, two-speed wipers, screen washers, cigarette lighter, and full wheel trims with rim finishers. Optional extras: radio, clock, revolution counter, Laycock overdrive, reversing light, exterior mirrors, overriders, and more.

COLOURS (1962): Saloon/convertible: two-tone, main body colour first, second is side flash and saloon roof, Pearl grey/Pippin red with Pippin red hood, Velvet green/Sage green with Sage green hood, Quartz blue metallic/Moonstone with blue hood, Solent blue metallic/Moonstone (saloon) or Solent blue metallic/Black with black hood (convertible). Single tones, all metallics, Steel grey with Pippin red hood, Bronze with Morocco brown hood, Quartz blue with medium blue hood. All convertibles available with black hood.
ENGINE: Four-cylinder OHV, bore 81.5mm, stroke 76.2mm, 1592cc, maximum bhp 80.25 at 5100rpm, twin Zenith 36WIA carburettors.
GEARBOX: Four-speed, floor-mounted gear change, overdrive optional, synchromesh

Instrument layout.

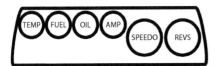

The car above has been fitted with side repeater indicators – a popular modification to 1960s cars, often carried out by 2nd or 3rd owners to bring them up to 1970s standards.

on top three gears. Ratios: top 4.22:1, 3rd 5.877:1, 2nd 9.038:1, 1st 14.128:1, reverse 17.896:1; with overdrive, o/d top 3.90, top 4.86, o/d 3rd 5.43, 3rd 6.76, 2nd 10.40, 1st 16.25, reverse 20.59.

REAR AXLE: Semi-floating, hypoid bevel, ratio 4.22:1, with overdrive 4.86:1.

BRAKES: Lockheed, front 10.81in discs, rear 9in drums.

TYRES: 5.60 x 15.

SUSPENSION: Front independent coil, rear semi-elliptic leaf springs, telescopic shock absorbers all round.

STEERING: Burman recirculating ball.

DIMENSIONS: Length: 13ft 6.5in (4128mm); **width:** 5ft 0.75in (1543mm); **height:** saloon 4ft 10in (1473mm), convertible 4ft 9.5in (1460mm); **weight:** saloon 1 ton 1cwt 0qtr 8lb (1070kg, dry 1021kg), convertible 5lb less (1068kg); **turning circle:** 36ft (11m).

CAPACITIES: Fuel 10 gallons (45 litres). Boot 13.5ft^3 (0.4m^3).

Floor gear change layout.

Rapier fronts:
Left: series 2; right: 3 and 3a;
below: 4 and 5.

Sunbeam Rapier series 4

Introduced in 1963 in saloon form only, the original intention had been to replace the Rapier with an all-new model along the lines of the Super-Minx, but the new Rapier became the Humber Sceptre. Just as the Minx remained in modified form, so did the Rapier, with revised front and rear end styling, narrower side flash, 13in wheels, modified suspension using sealed for life components, elimination of all greasing points, the glovebox was repositioned, and a parcel shelf added to the passenger side. Standard equipment now included heater, oil pressure gauge, ammeter, revolution counter, two-speed wipers, screen washers, headlamp flasher, cigarette lighter, front seats adjustable for reach and rake, adjustable telescopic steering column, power assisted brakes with discs at the front, reversing light, rubber faced overriders, and wheel trims.

COLOURS (1964): Two-tone, first is main body colour and second is side flash and roof, Autumn gold metallic/Embassy black, Light green metallic/Embassy black, Silver grey metallic/Embassy black, Quartz blue metallic/Moonstone, Moonstone/Quartz blue metallic. Two-tone, first is main body colour, second is side flash ONLY, Goodwood green metallic/Embassy black, Silver grey metallic/Pippin red, Pippin red/Embassy black. Single tone, Royal blue metallic.
ENGINE: Four-cylinder OHV, bore 81.5mm,

Instrument layout.

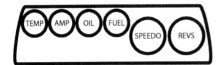

stroke 76.2mm, 1592cc, maximum bhp 84 at 5000rpm, Solex 32PAIA twin choke carburettor.

GEARBOX: Four-speed, floor-mounted gear change, overdrive optional, synchromesh on all forward gears. Ratios: at launch (later models as series 5), top 3.89:1, 3rd 5.413:1, 2nd 8.326:1, 1st 13.01:1, reverse 16.48:1; with overdrive, o/d top 3.39, top 4.22, o/d 3rd 4.71, 3rd 5.88, 2nd 9.04, 1st 14.13, reverse 17.9.

REAR AXLE: Semi-floating, hypoid bevel, ratio 3.89:1, with overdrive 4.22:1.

BRAKES: Lockheed, power assisted, front 10.3in discs, rear 9in drums.

TYRES: 6.00 x 13.

SUSPENSION: Front independent coil, rear semi-elliptic leaf springs, telescopic shock absorbers all round.

STEERING: Burman recirculating ball with adjustable telescopic steering column.

DIMENSIONS: Length: 13ft 7in (4140mm); **width:** 5ft 0.75in (1543mm); **height:** 4ft 9.75in (1461mm); **weight:** 1 ton 0cwt 3qtr 11lb (1059kg); **turning circle:** 36ft (11m).

CAPACITIES: Fuel tank 10 gallons (45 litres). Boot 13.5ft³ (0.4m³).

DIMENSIONS: Length: 13ft 7in (4140mm); **width:** 5ft 0.75in (1543mm); **height:** 4ft 9.75in (1461mm); **weight:** 1 ton 0cwt 3qtr 11lb (1059kg); **turning circle:** 36ft (11m).

CAPACITIES: Fuel 10 gallons (45 litres). Boot 13.5ft³ (0.4m³).

The car below has a stick-on rear screen demister, a popular accessory before the introduction of heated rear windscreens.

Floor gear change layout.

Sheepskin seat covers, padded steering wheel cover, rubber floor mats – this was customising in true 1960's style.

Sunbeam Rapier series 5

Introduced in 1965, the series 5 was the final version of this body style. Once again the power increased, thanks to a 175cc engine, and an alternator replaced the dynamo. It was discontinued in June 1967. Standard equipment included heater, oil pressure gauge, ammeter, revolution counter, two-speed wipers, screen washers, headlamp flasher, cigarette lighter, front seats adjustable for rake and reach, adjustable telescopic steering column, power assisted brakes with discs at front, reversing light, rubber faced overriders, and wheel trims. Optional extras: radio, clock, Laycock overdrive, whitewall tyres, and more.

COLOURS (1965-1966): Two-tone, main body colour first, second is side flash and roof. Autumn gold metallic/Embassy black, Silver grey metallic/Embassy black, Quartz blue metallic/Moonstone (1965 only). Two-tone, main body colour first, second is side flash ONLY, Silver grey metallic/Pippin red, Pippin red/Embassy black, Sherwood green metallic/Embassy black, Glade green metallic/Embassy black (1965 only), Lagoon blue metallic/Embassy black (1966 only). Single tones, Royal blue metallic. Laurel green metallic (1966 only).
ENGINE: Four-cylinder OHV, bore 81.5mm,

Instrument layout.

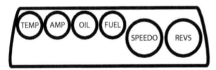

stroke 82.55mm, 1725cc, maximum bhp 85 at 5500rpm, Solex 32PAIAS twin choke carburettor.

GEARBOX: Four-speed, floor-mounted gear change, overdrive optional, synchromesh on all forward gears. Ratios: top 3.89:1, 3rd 5.413:1, 2nd 8.32:1, 1st 13.04:1, reverse 13.88:1; with overdrive, o/d top 3.39, top 4.22, o/d 3rd 4.9, 3rd 5.88, 2nd 9.2, 1st 14.16, reverse 15.06.

REAR AXLE: Semi-floating, hypoid bevel, ratio 3.89:1, with overdrive 4.22:1.

BRAKES: Lockheed, power assisted, front 10.3in discs, rear 9in drums.

TYRES: 6.00 x 13.

SUSPENSION: Front independent coil, rear semi-elliptic leaf springs, telescopic shock absorbers all round.

STEERING: Burman recirculating ball with 2.5in telescopic adjustment of steering column.

DIMENSIONS: Length: 13ft 7in (4140mm); **width:** 5ft 0.75in (1543mm); **height:** 4ft 9.5in (1461mm); **weight:** 1 ton 1cwt (1067kg); **turning circle:** 36ft (11m).

CAPACITIES: Fuel 10 gallons (45 litres). Boot 13.5ft^3 (0.4m^3).

Floor gear change layout.

Rapier rear wing trims:
top left: series 1; top right: series 2;
bottom left: series 3 and 3a;
bottom right: series 4 and 5.

Sunbeam Rapier (Arrow type)

Produced from 1967 until 1976 and using the underpan and chassis of the new Hunter/Vogue family, the new Rapier had a two-door Coupé bodywork unlike anything else in the Arrow range. Like the previous Minx-based Rapier it had a lengthy run, but this time there were not the regular face-lifts or engine changes, although in October 1968 a higher performance version the H120 was introduced. It was distinguished by its side stripes, black front grille and scooped boot lid which formed a spoiler at its top edge. The H in H120 is for Holbay, and the engine used in the Rapier H120 was also used in the Hunter GLS. Standard equipment (1968): heater/ventilation equipment with two-speed blower, opening front quarter lights, clock, oil pressure gauge, ammeter, revolution counter, two-speed wipers, screen washer, headlamp flasher, dipping interior mirror, cigarette lighter, reclining front seats, overdrive, reversing lights, overriders, wheel cover discs, (Rostyle wheels on H120), and more. Optional extras: radio, head rests, seat belts, Borg-Warner automatic transmission, fog and spotlights, whitewall tyres, and more.

COLOURS (1967-1968): Included Embassy black, Oxford blue, Holly green, Signal red, Polar white, and metallics – Gunmetal, Turquoise blue, Sherwood green, Golden sand, Claret.
COLOURS (1975): Carib blue, Lavender, Sunflower, Apricot, Orange Blossom, Imperial red, Cherry, Magenta, Polar white, and metallics – Kingfisher, Peppermint, Pinewood, Champagne, Copperbeech.
ENGINE: Four-cylinder OHV, bore 81.5mm, stroke 82.55mm, 1725cc, maximum bhp 88 at 5200rpm, later cars 92 at 5500rpm. H120 105bhp at 5200rpm, with twin Weber 40DCOE carburettors.

Instrument layout.

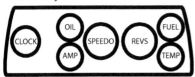

Below is a Sunbeam Alpine, introduced in 1969 and discontinued in 1975. It had a less powerful engine than the Rapier, and lacked some of the Rapier's standard equipment and instrumentation. The Alpine can be distinguished from the Rapier by its different rear boot trim, plain painted rear pillars, and lack of stainless steel sill covers.

ENGINE: Four-cylinder OHV, bore 81.5mm, stroke 82.55mm, 1725cc, maximum bhp 74 at 5500rpm, 82bhp at 5300rpm (1972), single Zenith/Stromberg carburettor.

Floor gear change layout, manual on left, automatic on right.

GEARBOX: Four-speed, floor-mounted gear change, with overdrive on top and third, optional three-speed automatic available (not H120), all synchromesh gearbox. Ratios: o/d top 3.39, top 4.22, o/d 3rd 4.39, 3rd 5.47, 2nd 8.41, 1st 13.18, reverse 14.03; H120 o/d top 3.12:1, top 3.89:1, o/d 3rd 4.05:1, 3rd 5.04:1, 2nd 7.75:1, 1st 12.14:1, reverse 12.92:1

REAR AXLE: Hypoid bevel, ratios: manual 4.22:1, automatic 3.70, H120 3.89:1.

BRAKES: Lockheed, power assisted, front 9.6 inch discs, rear 9 inch drums.

TYRES: Rapier 155 x 13, later 165 x 13, H120 165 x 13.

SUSPENSION: Front MacPherson strut, rear

Hillman estate and Sunbeam Rapier had the same rear lights.

semi-elliptic leaf springs, and telescopic shock absorbers.
STEERING: Recirculating ball.
DIMENSIONS: Length: 14ft 6.5in (4432mm); **width:** 5ft 4.75in (1586mm); **height:** 4ft 7in (1397mm); **weight:** 1 ton 0cwt 1qtr 7lb (1032kg), H120 20lb (9kg) more; **turning circle:** 33ft 6in (10.2m).
CAPACITIES: Fuel 15 gallons (68 litres). Boot 19ft³ (6m³).

Sunbeam Alpine

Produced from 1953 to 1955, the Sunbeam Alpine was basically a two-seater Sunbeam Talbot 90. The sports car, as most of us recognise it, was yet to come in the form of the 1959 Alpine. These early Alpines did enjoy some motorsport success, although it was the saloon cars that were used for most events, including the Monte Carlo rally. Mark 3s can be recognised by red rear lights, and the revolution counter incorporated into the dash, rather than being a separate add on accessory. There was no mark 2 model, the original mark 1 being based on the Sunbeam Talbot mark 2. Standard equipment included revolution counter, two-speed wipers, overdrive (optional on early cars), overriders, rim finishers, and tool kit. Optional extras: heater, radio, whitewall tyres, and more.

COLOURS: Ivory, Alpine mist, Sapphire blue, Coronation red.
ENGINE: Four-cylinder OHV, bore 81mm, stroke 110mm, 2267cc, maximum bhp 80 at 4200rpm, Stromberg carburettor, DAA36 (mark 1), DI36 (mark 3).
GEARBOX: Four-speed, steering column gear change, overdrive standard from late 1954,

Above: mark 1 dashboard. Note the position of the revolution counter on early cars.

Steering column gear change layout.

Early models previous page and above; later versions below. Some cars have been fitted with non-standard amber indicators.

synchromesh on top three gears. Ratios: o/d top 3.28:1, top 3.90:1, 3rd 5.19:1, 2nd 8.54:1, 1st 11.04:1, reverse 13.96:1.

REAR AXLE: Hypoid bevel, ratio 3.90:1, with overdrive 4.22:1.

BRAKES: Lockheed, front and rear 10in drums.

TYRES: 5.50 x 16.

SUSPENSION: Front independent coil, rear semi-elliptic leaf springs.

STEERING: Burman recirculating ball.

DIMENSIONS: Length: 14ft (4267mm); **width:** 5ft 2.5in (1588mm); **height:** 4ft 8in (1422mm); **weight:** 1 ton 5cwt 3qtr 16lb (1315kg).

CAPACITIES: Fuel 10 gallons (45 litres).

Note: floor-mounted gear change as on left, and just visible in the picture below, was a Sunbeam Talbot dealer-fitted conversion.

Instrument layout.

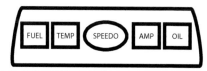

Optional floor-mounted gear lever.

Sunbeam Alpine series 1

Introduced in 1959, and based on the Hillman Husky underpan, the series 1 shared most of its running gear with the Sunbeam Rapier which had already demonstrated its ability as a successful rally car, winning the 1958 RAC Rally and taking 1st in class in the Monte Carlo and French Alpine Rallies. The 1959 retail price was £1032, while an Austin Healey Sprite with a 948cc engine was £632. Standard equipment included oil pressure gauge, revolution counter, front disc brakes, and rim finishers. Optional extras: heater, clock, ammeter, radio, Laycock overdrive, whitewall tyres, wire wheels, hard top, tonneau cover, and more.

COLOURS (1959): Carnival red, Thistle grey, Glen green, Embassy black, Moonstone. All soft/hard tops in black.
ENGINE: Four-cylinder OHV, bore 79mm, stroke 76.2mm, 1494cc, maximum bhp 78 at 5300rpm, twin Zenith 36WIP2 carburettors.
GEARBOX: Four-speed, floor-mounted gear change, overdrive optional, synchromesh on top three gears. Ratios: top 3.89:1, 3rd 5.413:1, 2nd 8.324:1, 1st 13.04:1, 16.48:1; with overdrive, o/d top 3.39, top 4.22, o/d 3rd 4.72, 3rd 5.877, 2nd 9.038, 1st 14.128, reverse 17.896.

REAR AXLE: Semi-floating, hypoid bevel, ratio 3.89:1, with overdrive 4.22:1.
BRAKES: Girling, front 9.5in discs, rear 9in drums.
TYRES: 5.60 x 13.
SUSPENSION: Front independent coil and telescopic shock absorbers, rear semi-elliptic leaf springs and lever arm shock absorbers.
STEERING: Burman recirculating ball.

DIMENSIONS: Length: 12ft 11.25in (3943mm); **width:** 5ft 0.5in (1537mm); **height:** 4ft 3.5in (1308mm); **weight:** 19cwt 0cwt 0qtr 8lb (969kg).
CAPACITIES: Fuel 9 gallons (41 litres).

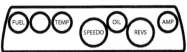

Floor gear change layout.

Instrument layout.

Sunbeam Alpine series 2

Introduced in 1960, and visually similar to the series 1, the series 2 had a full height window guide in the leading edge of the front doors, an interior light, and a 1592cc engine. Standard equipment included oil pressure gauge, revolution counter, interior light, central armrest with lockable storage box, front disc brakes, and rim finishers. Optional extras: heater, radio, Laycock overdrive, reversing lights, whitewall tyres, wire wheels, hard top, tonneau cover, and more.

COLOURS (1961): Carnival red, Moonstone, Lake blue, Wedgwood blue, Seacrest green. All soft/hard tops in black.

ENGINE: Four-cylinder OHV, bore 81.5mm, stroke 76.2mm, 1592cc, maximum bhp 85.5 at 5000rpm, twin Zenith 36WIP2 carburettors.

GEARBOX: Four-speed, floor-mounted gear change, overdrive optional, synchromesh on top three gears. Ratios: top 3.89:1, 3rd 5.413:1, 2nd 8.324:1, 1st 13.013:1, reverse 16.483:1; with overdrive, o/d top 3.39, top 4.22, o/d 3rd 4.72, 3rd 5.88, 2nd 9.04, 1st 14.13, reverse 17.9.

REAR AXLE: Semi-floating, hypoid bevel, ratio 3.89:1, with overdrive 4.22:1.

BRAKES: Girling, front 9.5in discs, rear 9in drums.

TYRES: 5.90 x 13.

SUSPENSION: Front independent coil and telescopic shock absorbers, rear semi-elliptic leaf springs and lever arm shock absorbers.

STEERING: Burman recirculating ball.

DIMENSIONS: Length: 12ft 11.25in (3943mm); **width:** 5ft 0.5in (1537mm); **height:** 4ft 3.5in (1308mm); **weight:** 19cwt 1qtr 9lb (982kg, dry 944kg); **turning circle:** 34ft (10.4m).

CAPACITIES: Fuel 9.5 gallons (43 litres). Boot 7ft^3 (2m^3).

Floor gear change layout.

Harrington Sunbeam Alpine
(Series 2 based)

Introduced in 1961, the original Harrington featured a moulded glass fibre top, which gave the appearance of simply bolting on over the original cabin and boot, although there was a lot more to it than that. The second generation Harrington, known as the Le Mans, had a more coach-built look to it. A final version, keeping the original rear wings but featuring the opening hatch of the Le Mans, arrived in 1962. The Harrington was discontinued in 1963. Optional extras: overdrive, oil cooler, power assisted steering, and more.

COLOURS: Varied according to manufacturer, due to being manufactured in 'kit-car' form.
ENGINE: Four-cylinder OHV, bore 81.5mm, stroke 76.2mm, 1592cc, maximum bhp 85.5 at 5000rpm, twin Zenith carburettors. *Note: various stages of tune were available as options but the original Alpine engine was normally fitted as standard.*
GEARBOX: Four-speed, floor-mounted gear change, overdrive optional, synchromesh on top three gears. Ratios: top 3.89:1, 3rd 5.413:1, 2nd 8.324:1, 1st 13.013:1, reverse 16.483:1.
REAR AXLE: Semi-floating, hypoid bevel, ratio 3.89:1.
BRAKES: Girling, front 9.5in discs, rear 9in drums.
TYRES: 5.90 x 13.
SUSPENSION: Front independent coil, rear semi-elliptic leaf springs.
STEERING: Recirculating ball.
DIMENSIONS: Length: 12ft 11.25in (3943mm); **width:** 5ft 0.5in (1537mm); **height:** 4ft 3.5in (1308mm); **weight:** 19cwt 3qtr 2lb (993kg); **turning circle:** 34ft (10.4m).
CAPACITIES: Fuel 9.5 gallons (43 litres). Boot 7ft³ (2m³).

Floor gear change layout.

Sunbeam Alpine series 3

Introduced in 1963, this season's changes included repositioning the spare wheel to fit upright in the boot, and twin upright fuel tanks, thus providing a more useable space for luggage. Added to the range was a GT model with standard body-coloured hardtop, wood-rimmed steering wheel, and walnut-veneered dashboard. Also new were an adjustable telescopic steering column and two-speed wipers. Externally, quarter lights in the front doors differentiated it from the series 2. Optional extras: heater (standard on GT), radio, clock, cigarette lighter, seat belts, laminated windscreen, Laycock overdrive, reversing lights, whitewall tyres, wire wheels, hard top, tonneau cover, and more.

COLOURS (1963): Carnival red, Moonstone, Wedgewood blue, and metallics – Light green, Quartz blue, Autumn gold. All soft/hard tops in black except GT model.

ENGINE: Four cylinder OHV, bore 81.5mm, stroke 76.2mm, 1592cc, Tourer – maximum bhp 82 at 5200rpm, twin Zenith 36WIP3 carburettors, GT – 77bhp at 5000rpm, twin Zenith 36WIA3, (all late 1963 models Solex 32PAIA).

GEARBOX: Four-speed, floor-mounted gear change, overdrive optional, synchromesh on top three gears. Ratios: o/d top 3.12:1, top 3.89:1, o/d 3rd 3.85:1, 3rd 4.80:1, 2nd 7.38:1, 1st 11.53:1, reverse 14.61:1.

REAR AXLE: Semi-floating hypoid bevel, ratio 3.89:1 with or without overdrive.

BRAKES: Girling, front 9.85in discs, rear 9in drums.

TYRES: 5.90 x 13.

SUSPENSION: Front independent coil, rear semi-elliptic leaf springs, telescopic shock absorbers all round.

STEERING: Burman recirculating ball with adjustable telescopic steering column.

DIMENSIONS: Length: 12ft 11.25in (3943mm); **width:** 5ft 0.5in (1537mm); **height:** Tourer 4ft 3.5in (1308mm), GT 4ft 4.5in (1334mm); **weight:** Tourer 19cwt 3qtr 8lb (1007kg), GT 1 ton (1016kg); **turning circle:** 34ft (10.4 m).

CAPACITIES: Fuel 11.25 gallons (51 litres). Boot 9.7ft^3 (0.3m^3).

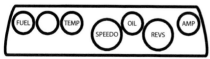

Instrument layout.

Sunbeam Alpine series 4

Introduced in 1964, this car had revised body styling with trimmed down rear fins and new front grille. Brochures show the Touring model with a black dashboard, but some have walnut-veneered dashboards. Standard equipment: oil pressure gauge, revolution counter, two-speed wipers, windscreen washers, headlamp flasher, adjustable telescopic steering column, reclining front seats, power assisted brakes with discs at front. Optional extras: heater (standard on GT), radio, clock, seat belts, laminated windscreen, Laycock, overdrive or Borg-Warner automatic transmission, reversing lights, wire wheels, tonneau cover, and more.

COLOURS (1964): Carnival red, Moonstone, Wedgewood blue, Forest green, Midnight blue, Balmoral grey. All soft/hard tops in black except GT model.
ENGINE: Four-cylinder OHV, bore 81.5mm, stroke 76.2mm, 1592cc, maximum bhp 80.5 at 5000rpm, single Solex 32PAIA compound carburettor, (Tourer and GT models).
GEARBOX: Four-speed, floor-mounted gear change, overdrive or automatic optional, synchromesh on all forward gears. Ratios: top 3.89:1, 3rd 5.413:1, 2nd 8.324:1, 1st 13.013:1, reverse 16.483:1; with automatic, top 3.89:1, 2nd 5.64:1, 1st 9.31:1, reverse 8.14:1.
REAR AXLE: Semi-floating, hypoid bevel, ratio with or without automatic 3.89:1, with overdrive 4.22:1.
BRAKES: Girling, power assisted, front 9.85in discs, rear 9in drums.
TYRES: 6.00 x 13.
SUSPENSION: Front independent coil, rear semi-elliptic leaf springs, telescopic shock absorbers all round.
STEERING: Burman recirculating ball with 2.5in telescopic adjustment of steering column.
DIMENSIONS: **Length**: 12ft 11.25in (3943mm); **width**: 5ft 0.5in (1537mm); **height**: 4ft 3.5in (1308mm); **weight**: 19cwt 3qtr 8lb (1007kg); **turning circle**: 34ft (10.4m).
CAPACITIES: Fuel 11.25 gallons (51 litres). Boot 9.7ft^3 (0.3m^3).

Floor gear change layouts, manual left and optional automatic on the right.

Sunbeam Alpine series 5

Introduced in 1965, with an enlarged engine of 1725cc and an alternator to replace the dynamo, the automatic option was now deleted. A 1966 brochure demonstrates adjustable pedals as well as the steering column. This was to be the last true sports car produced by Rootes, as it was discontinued in January 1968, and all following Alpines being family saloons. The 1967 retail price for the convertible was £948; an MGB was £919. Standard equipment included oil pressure gauge, revolution counter, central armrest with lockable storage box, two-speed wipers, windscreen washers, headlamp flasher, adjustable telescopic steering column, and power assisted brakes with discs at front. Optional extras: heater (standard on GT), radio, clock, seat belts, laminated windscreen, Laycock overdrive, reversing lights, wire wheels, tonneau cover, and more.

COLOURS (1965/1966): (1965 only*, 1966 only†). Carnival red, Mediterranean blue, British racing green, Midnight blue* Artic white* Jet black*. Commodore blue† Polar white† Orchid green† All soft/hard tops in black except GT model.
ENGINE: Four-cylinder OHV, bore 81.5mm, stroke 82.55mm, capacity 1725cc, maximum bhp 92.5 at 5500rpm, twin Stromberg 150CD carburettors, (Tourer and GT).
GEARBOX: Four-speed, floor-mounted gear change, overdrive optional, synchromesh on all forward gears. Ratios: top 3.89:1, 3rd 5.04:1, 2nd 7.74:1, 1st 12.14:1, reverse 13.01:1; with overdrive, o/d top 3.39, top 4.22, o/d 3rd 4.39, 3rd 5.47, 2nd 8.40, 1st 13.17, reverse 14.01.
REAR AXLE: Semi-floating, hypoid bevel, ratio 3.89:1, with overdrive 4.22:1.
BRAKES: Girling, power assisted, front 9.85in discs, rear 9in drums.
TYRES: 6.00 x 13.
SUSPENSION: Front independent coil, rear semi-elliptic leaf springs, telescopic shock absorbers all round.
STEERING: Burman recirculating ball with 2.5in telescopic adjustment of steering column.
DIMENSIONS: Length: 12ft 11.25in (3943mm); **width:** 5ft 0.5in (1537mm);

height: 4ft 3.5in (1308mm); **weight:** 19cwt 2qtr 16lb (1007kg).
CAPACITIES: Fuel 11.25 gallons (51 litres). Boot 9.5ft³ (0.3m³).

Floor gear change layout.

Instrument layout.

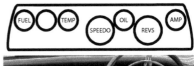

Sunbeam Tiger

Perhaps spurned on by the success of the AC Cobra, Rootes decided to put a Ford V8 into its Alpine IV, the result, the Sunbeam Tiger, launched in 1964. Unfortunately, when Chrysler took over it did not have a suitable engine to replace the Ford unit, and using a competitor's engine was probably going to cause problems, so unfortunately the Tiger had a relatively short life. Maybe the lack of any real visual difference from its less powerful sibling, the Alpine, did not help either. Standard equipment included rally seats, adjustable steering column and pedals, and power assisted brakes.

COLOURS (1965): Carnival red, Midnight blue, Mediterranean blue, Artic white, British racing green, Jet black. All soft/hard tops in black, hard tops available in body colour if specified as factory fitted optional extra.

All cars on this page are Sunbeam Tiger 1.

Instrument layout.

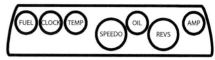

Floor gear change layout.

Sunbeam Tiger 1 (1964 to 1966)

ENGINE: Ford V8 OHV, bore 96.5mm, stroke 73mm, 4261cc, (260 ci), maximum bhp 164 at 4400rpm, Ford twin choke carburettor.

GEARBOX: Four-speed, synchromesh on all forward gears. Ratios: top 2.88:1, 3rd 3.71:1 2nd 4.86:1 1st 6.68:1 reverse 6.68:1.

REAR AXLE: Hypoid, ratio 2.88:1.

BRAKES: Power assisted, front 9.85in discs, rear 9in drums.

TYRES: 5.90 x 13.

SUSPENSION: Front independent coil, rear semi-elliptic leaf springs with Panhard rod.

STEERING: Rack and pinion.

DIMENSIONS: Length: 13ft 2in (4013mm); **width:** 5ft 0.5in (1537mm); **height:** 4ft 3.5in (1308mm); **weight:** Tiger 1 – Tourer, 1 ton 2cwt 1qtr 5lb (1145kg), coupé 1 ton 3cwt 0qtr 0lb (1168kg), Tiger 2 – add 45lb (20kg); **turning circle:** 37.5ft (11.6m).

CAPACITIES: Fuel 11.25 gallons (51 litres). Boot 9.7ft^3 (0.3m^3).

Sunbeam Tiger 2

If the life of the Tiger 1 was short (1964-1966), then the lifespan of the Tiger 2, at less than a year (1967), was back to the good old days when Rootes updated its cars annually. It can be identified from the Tiger 1 by its different grille and side stripes. Technical differences: see below.

ENGINE: Ford V8 OHV, bore 101.6mm,stroke 73mm, 4727cc (289ci), maximum bhp 200 at 4400rpm.
GEARBOX: Four-speed, all synchromesh. Ratios: top 2.88:1, 3rd 3.92:1, 2nd 5.56:1, 1st 8.01:1, reverse 8.01:1.

Sunbeam Imp Sport

Introduced in 1966, three years after the Hillman Imp on which it was based, the Sunbeam Imp provided Rootes with its third variant to compliment the Singer Chamois and the Hillman Imp. The Sunbeam Imp was variously named as the Sunbeam Imp Sport or simply the Sunbeam Sport. Considering it had a ten year run until 1976 these cars seem very scarce – perhaps as they matured they fell into the hands of individuals who raced/rallied them into the ground. Standard equipment included heater and blower, ammeter, windscreen washers, headlamp flasher, twin tone horn, fully reclining front seats, and wheel cover discs. Note: a voltmeter replaced the ammeter on later cars, and the Stiletto was fitted with a revolution counter instead of an ammeter or voltmeter. Optional extras: radio, seat belts, reversing light, overriders, and more.

During 1968 the Imp Sport adopted the revised front end styling of the Hillman Super Imp (see right, this is actually a Sunbeam Californian), and then, in 1970, the Imp Sport became the Sport, with twin headlamps as first seen on the Singer Chamois in 1968. The front end of the model immediately below is like that of the Singer, possibly a re-badged version following the deletion of the Singer range in 1970, the green model below that has the more traditional Sunbeam front trim.

Instrument layout for 1973 Imp.

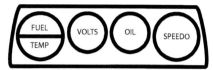

COLOURS (1966 Sunbeam Imp Sport): Signal red, Ming blue, Polar white, Lincoln green, Golden bronze.
COLOURS (1975 Sunbeam Sport): Polar white, Apricot, Orange blossom, Cherry, Magenta, Sunflower, Imperial red, Carib blue, and metallics, Champagne, Peppermint, Pinewood, Kingfisher, Copperbeech.
ENGINE: Four-cylinder OHV (rear-mounted) bore 68mm, stroke 60.35mm, 875cc maximum bhp 51 at 6100rpm, twin Stromberg 125CD carburettors.
GEARBOX/REAR AXLE: Four-speed, floor-mounted gear change, all synchromesh gearbox combined with hypoid bevel transaxle. Ratios: top 4.138:1, 3rd 5.702:1, 2nd 8.905:1, 1st 16.595:1, reverse 13.824:1.
BRAKES: Girling, power assisted, front and rear 8in drums.
TYRES: 155 x 12.

Floor gear change layout.

SUSPENSION: Front independent coil/swing axle, rear independent coil/trailing links.
STEERING: Rack and pinion.

The Sunbeam Stiletto coupé was only produced from 1967 until 1973, standard equipment was slightly different to the Sunbeam Imp and Imp Sport, and included revolution counter, fold down rear seats, and vinyl roof covering.

DIMENSIONS: Length: 11ft 7in (3531mm); **width:** 5ft 0.75in (1543mm); **height:** 4ft 6.5in (1384mm); **weight:** 14cwt 2qtr 9lb (741kg); **turning circle:** 30ft 6in (9.3m).
CAPACITIES: Fuel 6 gallons (27 litres). Boot: front 3.25ft³, rear 5ft³, or 16.5ft³ with seat lowered (combined 0.25 or 0.6m³).

Instrument layout for 1968 Stiletto.

Note: many cars on theses pages have non-standard wheels fitted: the red Imp, below, and the green and white Stilettos, on the right, have the original standard wheels fitted.

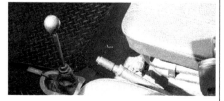

Above: Yes, that is the choke control in front of the gear lever!

Above: Early Imps had vents above the rear windows; later Imps did not.

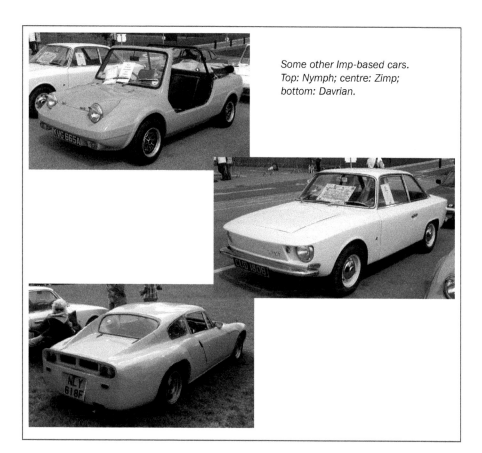

Some other Imp-based cars.
Top: Nymph; centre: Zimp;
bottom: Davrian.

Clan Crusader & Clan

The Clan Crusader was a fibreglass monocoque two-seater sports car, which used the Rootes Imp Sport engine and running gear. It was initially produced from 1971 until late 1973 when the company ran into financial difficulties and was available for a while in kit form as well as a completed car. Production was started again in 1982, the car being called simply 'the Clan,' it featured a restyled body with retractable headlamps, and a choice of two 998cc engines from Hartwell. In 1985 a mid-engined version using an Alfa Romeo engine was launched, but once again the company ran into financial difficulties and finally ceased trading in June 1987. Standard equipment included heater, two-speed wipers, screen washers, and power assisted brakes.

COLOURS: Not available, as they were produced in kit-car form, including self-assembly kits.
ENGINE (Crusader): Four-cylinder OHV (rear-mounted) bore 68mm, stroke 60.35mm, 875cc maximum bhp 51 at 6100rpm, twin Stromberg 125CDS carburettors.
GEARBOX/REAR AXLE: Four-speed, floor-mounted gear change, all synchromesh gearbox combined with hypoid bevel transaxle. Ratios: top 4.138:1, 3rd 5.702:1, 2nd 8.905:1, 1st 16.595:1, reverse 13.824:1, final drive ratio 4.86:1.
ENGINE (Clan "E" 65 bhp & "S" 78 bhp models): Four-cylinder OHV (rear-mounted) bore 72.54mm, stroke 60.375mm, 998cc, maximum bhp 65 or 78, twin Stromberg 150 CD or single Weber 40 DCOE carburettors.
BRAKES: Girling, power assisted, front and rear 8in drums (Crusader), front discs and rear drums (Clan).
TYRES: 155 x 12 (Crusader), 175 x 13 or 185 x 13 (Clan E & S).
SUSPENSION: Front independent coil springs, swing axle and telescopic dampers. Rear independent coil springs, trailing links and telescopic dampers.
STEERING: Rack and pinion.
DIMENSIONS: Crusader – **Length:** 12ft 6in (3810mm); **width:** 4ft 10.5in (1486mm); **height:** 3ft 7in (1092mm); **weight:** 11cwt 1qtr

The two models at top are Clan Crusader; the white cars above are Clan.

17lb (580kg); **turning circle:** approx 30ft (9.1 metres). Clan – as above, except: **Length:** 12ft 9in (3886mm); **weight:** 11cwt 1qtr 20lb (582kg).
CAPACITIES: Fuel 6 gallons (27 litres).

Ginetta G15 & G21

Another car that used the Imp Sport engine was the Ginetta G15. It was produced from 1968 to 1974, but, unlike the Clan, it used Triumph front suspension and steering, and had a tubular steel chassis. Ginetta had been producing cars since 1961 using Ford components, but used another Rootes engine – the Rapier H120 – for its G21 models produced from 1973 to 1978.

COLOURS: Not available – varied according to manufacturer, due to being manufactured in 'kit-car' form.
ENGINE (Ginetta G15): Four-cylinder OHV (rear-mounted) bore 68mm, stroke 60.35mm, 875cc maximum bhp 51 at 6100rpm, twin Stromberg carburettors.
GEARBOX/REAR AXLE: Four-speed, floor-mounted gear change, all synchromesh gearbox combined with hypoid bevel transaxle. Ratios: top 3.9:1, 3rd 5.8:1, 2nd 8.7:1, 1st 16.5:1, reverse 13.82:1, final drive ratio 4.86:1.
BRAKES (G15): Girling, power assisted, front 9in discs, rear 8in drums.
TYRES: 5.20 x 13.
SUSPENSION: Front independent coil springs, wishbones, anti-roll bar and telescopic dampers. Rear independent coil springs, trailing links and telescopic dampers.
STEERING: Rack and pinion.
DIMENSIONS: G15 – Length: 12ft 2in (3708mm); width: 4ft 8.5in (1435mm); height: 3ft 8.5in (1130mm); weight: 11cwt (559kg); turning circle: approx 30ft (9.1m).
CAPACITIES: Fuel 6 gallons (27 litres).
ENGINE (Ginetta G21S): Four-cylinder OHV bore 81.5mm, stroke 82.5mm, 1725cc maximum bhp 98 at 4000rpm, twin Weber 40 DCOE carburettors.
GEARBOX: Four-speed, floor-mounted gear change, all synchromesh gearbox. Ratios: o/d top 2.97:1, top 3.7:1, o/d 3rd 3.85, 3rd 4.8:1, 2nd 7.37:1, 1st 11.55:1.
REAR AXLE: Hypoid bevel, ratio 3.71.
BRAKES (G21S): Girling, power assisted, front 9.6 inch discs, rear 9 inch drums.
TYRES: 185/70 x 13.
SUSPENSION: Front double wishbones, anti-roll bar, and telescopic dampers. Rear

The models above are Ginetta G15, the model below and on the next page are Ginetta G21.

independent coil springs, radius arms and telescopic dampers.
STEERING: Rack and pinion.
DIMENSIONS: G21S – **Length:** 13ft 5in (4089mm); **width:** 5ft 3in (1600mm); **height:** 3ft 10in (1168mm); **turning circle:** approx 30ft (9.1 metres); **weight:** 16cwt (1023kg).
CAPACITIES: Fuel 10 gallons (45 litres), boot 6.3ft^3 (0.2m^3).

Sunbeam Venezia

The Venezia is included here because it could have so easily have become the new Rapier of 1963. It was based on the under-frame of the Humber Sceptre, which had itself started life as the intended replacement for the Rapier. The Venezia was built by Carrozzeria Touring of Milan between 1963 and 1966. The car was destined initially for the Italian market, with exports to other European countries planned, but they are rarely found in the UK.

COLOURS: Varied according to manufacturer.
ENGINE: Rootes own as used in the Rapier. Four-cylinder OHV, bore 81.5mm, stroke 76.2mm, 1592cc, maximum bhp 88 at 5500rpm, Solex twin choke carburettor.
GEARBOX: Four-speed with overdrive. Ratios: o/d top 3.39:1, top 4.22:1, o/d 3rd 4.72:1,

3rd 5.88:1, 2nd 9.04:1, 1st 14.13:1, reverse 17.9:1.
REAR AXLE: Semi-floating, hypoid bevel, ratio 4.22:1.
BRAKES: Lockheed, power-assisted, front 10.3in discs, rear 9in drums.
TYRES: 6.00 x 13.
SUSPENSION: Front independent coil, rear semi-elliptic leaf springs.
STEERING: Burman recirculating ball.
DIMENSIONS: Length: 14ft 8.8in (4491mm); **width:** 5ft 1.4in (1560mm); **height:** 4ft 5.9in (1369mm); **weight:** 1 ton 2cwt 0qtr 11lb (1123kg).

Instrument layout.

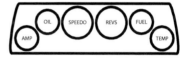

For some overseas markets the Sunbeam name was used instead of Hillman and Singer – see below, and pictures on following page.

Sunbeam Arrow.

The Arrow range of cars were badged as Sunbeams for Europe, the USA and Canada as follows:

Hillman Minx, UK = Sunbeam Minx, Europe and Sunbeam Arrow, Canada.
Hillman Estate, UK = Sunbeam Estate, Europe and Sunbeam Arrow Estate, Canada/USA.
Hillman Hunter UK = Sunbeam Hunter, Europe and Sunbeam Arrow, USA.
Singer Gazelle, UK = Sunbeam Gazelle, Europe.
Singer Vogue, UK = Sunbeam Vogue, Europe.
Singer Vogue Estate, UK = Sunbeam Vogue Estate, Europe.

Sunbeam Avenger.

Sunbeam Chamois.

Sunbeam Californian.

Plymouth Cricket – the name given to the Hillman Avenger sold in America.

www.velocebooks.com / www.veloce.co.uk
All current books • New book news • Special offers • Gift vouchers

Chrysler 180/2 Litre

The 180 was introduced in 1971 and the 2 Litre followed in 1973. Chrysler's original intention during development had been to use this car to replace all of the larger Humbers, and provide Simca with a large car. However, the Humber version was subsequently cancelled, leaving the Simca-engined car as the only version to be produced. Incidentally, all the large Humbers had been discontinued in 1967. The engines became OHC instead of OHV in 1976. Both 180 and 2 Litre models were discontinued in 1979. Retail prices, 180: 1971 £1499, 1973 £1662, 1979 £3949; 2 Litre: automatic 1973 £1932, 1979 £4700. A 1979 Ford Cortina 2000 GL, which was the same size, cost £3932. Standard equipment both models (1977): clock, revolution counter, cigar lighter, reclining front seats, seat belts, front seat headrests, heated rear window, reversing lights, auxiliary driving lights, Halogen headlamps, overriders, door mirror, vinyl roof, and more.

COLOURS (1976): Polar white, Champagne, Gold dust, Sunflower, Apricot, Copperbeech, Cherry, Peppermint, Pinewood, Lavender, Kingfisher.

The red car above is a 180; the others are 2 Litre models.

ENGINE: 180 – four-cylinder OHV, bore 87.7mm, stroke 75mm, 1812cc, maximum bhp 100 at 5800rpm, Weber 38ADS carburettor, (from 1973 Weber 34ADSD). **2 Litre** – four-cylinder OHV, bore 91.7mm, stroke 75mm, 1981cc, maximum bhp 110 at 5800rpm, Weber 34ADSD carburettor.
GEARBOX: 180 – manual four-speed, ratios: top 1:1, 3rd 1.418:1, 2nd 2.175:1 1st 3.546:1, reverse 3.226:1. **2 Litre** – automatic three-speed, ratios: top 1:1, 2nd 1.45:1, 1st 2.45:1, reverse 2.2:1.
REAR AXLE: 180 – ratio 3.91:1, **2 Litre** – ratio 3.73:1.
BRAKES: Power assisted, front 9.8in discs, rear 9in discs.
TYRES: 175 x 14.
SUSPENSION: Front coil spring and strut, rear four link and coil spring, telescopic shock absorbers front and rear.
STEERING: Rack and pinion.
DIMENSIONS: Length: 14ft 10.2in (4527mm); **width:** 5ft 8in (1728mm); **height:**

4ft 9.1in (1450mm); **weight: 180** – 2418lb (1097kg), **2 Litre** – 2466lb (1119kg); **turning circle:** 34ft (10.3m).

153

Chrysler Alpine

Introduced in 1976, the first hatchback from Chrysler, the Alpine was known as the Simca 1307 and 1308 in France where it was assembled. In 1977 it was available in three model options, GL, S, and GLS. Retail prices: 1977 GL 1294cc £3072, 1979 GL 1294cc £3984, 1979 GL 1442cc £4544. S additional equipment over GL: halogen headlamps, centre console, rear compartment heating, load area light, etc. GLS: as S, plus headlamp wash/wipe, tinted glass, electric front windows, front seat headrests, and more.

COLOURS: Varied according to model.
ENGINES: All four-cylinder. GL – bore 76.7mm, stroke 70mm, 1294cc, maximum bhp 68 at 5600rpm, Solex 32BISA carburettor. S/GLS – bore 76.7mm, stroke 78mm, 1442cc, maximum bhp 85 at 5600rpm, Weber 36DCNV carburettor.
TRANSMISSION: Front-wheel drive, four-speed gearbox, floor-mounted gear change, synchromesh on all gears. Ratios: (1442) top 1.08:1, 3rd 1.52:1, 2nd 2.32:1, 1st 3.77:1, final drive 3.59:1.

The cars below have Chrysler badges on the bonnet and Simca badges on the rear tailgate; the car above has Chrysler badges front and rear.

BRAKES: Dual circuit, power assisted, front 9.5in disc, rear 9in drum.
TYRES: 155 x 13.
SUSPENSION: Front independent torsion bars, rear independent coil springs with front and rear anti-roll bars and shock absorbers all round.
STEERING: Rack and pinion.
DIMENSIONS: Length: 13ft 11.1in (4245mm); **width:** 5ft 6.1in (1680mm); **height:** 4ft 6.7in (1390mm); **weight:** GL 2315lb (1050kg), S 2359lb (1070kg), GLS 2370lb (1075kg); **turning circle:** 34ft (10.4m).
CAPACITIES: Fuel 13.2 gallons (60 litres). Boot 10.8ft^3, or 49ft^3 with rear seat folded down (0.3m^3 or 1.4m^3).

Talbot Alpine 1

The Alpine 1 was introduced in 1979, following Peugeot's acquisition of Chrysler's European operations, the range was revised and a new engine added. GLS standard equipment: radio/tape player, tailgate wash/wipe, velour upholstery, and more. SX adds: power steering, automatic transmission, headlamp wash/wipe, cruise control and multi function computer/calculator.

COLOURS: Ermine white, Cherry, Jonquil, Tartan green, Conifer green, Navy blue, Royal blue, Sweetcorn.
ENGINES: All four-cylinder. LS – bore 76.7mm, stroke 70mm, 1294cc, maximum bhp 67 at 5600rpm. LS/GL/GLS – bore 76.7mm, stroke 78mm, 1442cc, maximum bhp 84 at 5600rpm. SX – bore 80.6mm, stroke 78mm, 1592cc, maximum bhp 87 at 5400rpm.
TRANSMISSION: LS/GL/GLS – front-wheel drive, four-speed gearbox, floor-mounted gear change, synchromesh on all gears. Ratios: (1294) top 1.08:1, 3rd 1.52:1, 2nd 2.31:1, 1st 3.9:1, reverse 3.77:1, final drive 3.706:1, (1442) top 1.04:1, 3rd 1.52:1, 2nd 2.31:1, 1st 3.9:1, reverse 3.77:1, final drive 3.59:1. SX, front-wheel drive, three-speed automatic with floor-mounted selector. Ratios: top 1:1, 2nd 1.48:1, 1st 2.48:1, reverse 2.10:1, final drive 3.67:1.
BRAKES: Dual circuit, power assisted, front 9.5in disc, rear 9in drum.

TYRES: LS/GL 155 x 13, GLS/SX 165 x 13.
SUSPENSION: Front independent torsion bars, rear Independent coil springs with front and rear anti-roll bars, and shock absorbers all round.
STEERING: Rack and pinion, power assisted on SX.
DIMENSIONS: Length: 14ft 2in (4318mm); width: 5ft 6.1in (1680mm); height: 4ft 6.7in (1390mm); weight: LS 2293lb (1040kg), GL 2337lb (1060kg), GLS 2381lb (1080kg), SX 2447lb (1110kg); turning circle: 35ft (10.6m).
CAPACITIES: Fuel 12.75 gallons (58 litres). Boot 10.9ft^3 or 49ft^3 with rear seat folded down (0.3 or 1.4m^3).

Note: Some Chrysler Alpines may have been rebadged by dealers as Talbot models: they can be easily identified by the forward-sloping front grille and headlights.

Talbot Alpine 2

The Alpine 2, introduced in 1982 to replace the Talbot Alpine 1, was discontinued in 1986. The 1442cc engine was dropped in favour of the 1592cc engine, and 1984 would see the reintroduction of two familiar Rootes names – Minx and Rapier – which were applied to both the Alpine and Solara ranges.

COLOURS: Ermine white, Jonquil, Cherry, Baltic blue, Café noir, Embassy black, and metallics – Bluesteel, Peony, Silver, Gilt, Storm, Turbo green. Two-tones, upper body first – Café noir/Gilt, Peony/Silver, Embassy black/Silver, Bluesteel/Silver, Storm/Turbo green.

ENGINES: All four-cylinder. LE/LS/GL – bore 76.7mm, stroke 70mm, 1294cc, maximum bhp 67 at 5600rpm, Solex 32BISA or Weber 32IBSA carburettor. LE/LS/GL/GLS – bore 80.6mm, stroke 78mm, 1592cc, maximum bhp 89 at 5400rpm, Weber 36DCNV carburettor, or 36DCA (automatic model).

TRANSMISSION: Front-wheel drive, floor-mounted gear change/selector, synchromesh on all gears. 1294cc engine – four-speed gearbox. Ratios: top 1.086:1, 3rd 1.148:1, 2nd 1.88:1, 1st 3.308:1, reverse 3.33:1, final drive 4.786:1. 1592cc engine – five-speed gearbox. Ratios: top 0.757:1, 4th 0.969:1, 3rd 1.28:1, 2nd 1.88:1, 1st 3.308:1, reverse 3.33:1, final drive 4.187:1. GLS and GL with 1592cc engine, three-speed automatic optional.

All above: Alpine Rapier

BRAKES: Dual circuit, power assisted, front 9.5in disc, rear 9in drum.

TYRES: 155 x 13 with 1294cc engine, 165 x 13 with 1592cc engine.

SUSPENSION: Front independent torsion bars, rear independent coil springs with front and rear anti-roll bars and shock absorbers all round

STEERING: Rack and pinion, power assisted with 1592cc engine.

DIMENSIONS: Length: 14ft 2in (4318mm); **width:** 5ft 6.1in (1680mm); **height:** 4ft 6.7in (1390mm); **weights:** LE 2274lb (1031kg), LS 2321lb (1053kg), GL 2336lb (1060kg), GLS 2343lb (1063kg).

Instrument layout.

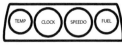

Talbot Solara 2

The Solara 2 was introduced in 1982 to replace the Solara 1. Minx and Rapier editions appeared in 1984, and the Solara was discontinued along with the rest of the Talbot range in 1986. Specifications below are for mid 1983.

The Talbot Solara 1 introduced in 1980 had all black front and rear 'bumpers.'

Above, Solara Rapier; below, Solara Minx.

COLOURS: As Talbot Alpine 2.

ENGINES: All four-cylinder. LE/LS/GL – bore 76.7mm, stroke 70mm, 1294cc, maximum bhp 67 at 5600rpm, Solex 32BISA carburettor. LE/LS/GL/GLS – bore 80.6mm, stroke 78mm, 1592cc, maximum bhp 87 at 5400rpm, Weber 36DCNV carburettor.

TRANSMISSION: Front-wheel drive, floor-mounted gear change/selector, synchromesh on all gears. 1294cc engine – four-speed gearbox, ratios: top 1.086:1, 3rd 1.148:1, 2nd 1.88:1, 1st 3.308:1, reverse 3.33:1, final drive 4.786:1. 1592cc engine – five-speed gearbox, ratios: top 0.757:1, 4th 0.969:1, 3rd 1.28:1, 2nd 1.88:1, 1st 3.308:1, reverse 3.33:1, final drive 4.187:1. LS/GL three-speed automatic optional.

BRAKES: Dual circuit, power assisted, front 9.5in disc, rear 9in drum.

TYRES: 155 x 13 with 1294cc engine, 165 x 13 with 1592cc engine.

SUSPENSION: Front independent torsion bars, rear independent coil springs with front and rear anti-roll bars and shock absorbers all round.

STEERING: Rack and pinion, power assisted with 1592cc engine (not LE).

DIMENSIONS: Length: 14ft 5in (4393mm); **width:** 5ft 6.1in (1680mm); **height:** 4ft 6.7in (1390mm); **weights:** LE 2202lb (999kg), LS 2254lb (1022kg), GL 2297lb (1042kg), GLS 2326lb (1055kg); **turning circle:** 35ft (10.6m). **CAPACITIES:** Fuel 12.75 gallons (58 litres). Boot 10.1ft³ (0.3m³).

Instrument layout.

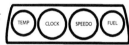

Floor gear change layout with five-speed gearbox.

157

Talbot Horizon 2

Introduced in 1983, the range was as follows: LE 1.1, LS 1.1 and 1.3, GL 1.5, GLS 1.5 and LD 1.9 (diesel), but by 1985, when it was discontinued, it had become LX, GLS and LD. The original Chrysler Horizon models were sold in America as the Dodge Omni and Plymouth Horizon, but used a 1.7-litre Volkswagen engine. LE standard equipment included reclining front seats, seat belts, folding rear seat, heated rear window, rear fog lights, hazard warning flashers, and two-speed wipers with flick wipe; LS added radio, front seat headrests, rear wash/wipe, and reversing lights; GL/GLS added Halogen headlamps, remote control drivers door mirror, cigar lighter, front door pockets, electric front windows (GLS only), and more.

COLOURS (1985): Antelope beige, Midnight blue, Cherry, Alpine white, Heather green, and metallics – Sable, Silver, Cascade blue, Peppermint, Pagoda red, Ming blue.
ENGINES: All four-cylinder. *(Note: all engines used both Solex and Weber carburettors).* LE/LS – bore 74mm, stroke 65mm, 1118cc, maximum bhp 58 at 5600rpm, Solex 32BISA or Weber 31IBSA carburettor. LX/LS (optional) – bore 76.7mm, stroke 70mm, 1294cc, maximum bhp 64 at 5600rpm, Solex 32BISA carburettor. GL/GLS – bore 76.7mm, stroke 78mm, 1442cc, maximum bhp 82 at 5600rpm, Weber 36DCNV carburettor. LD – bore 83mm, stroke 88mm, 1905cc, maximum bhp 64 at 4600rpm.

TRANSMISSION: Front-wheel drive, floor-mounted gear change, synchromesh on all gears. LE/LS/LD – four-speed, ratios: top 1.08:1, 3rd 1.52;1, 2nd 2.31:1, 1st 3.9:1, reverse 3.77:1, final drive (1118) 3.7:1, (1295) 3.59:1 or 3.47:1. GL/GLS – five-speed, ratios: top 0.757:1, 4th.969:1, 3rd 1.28:1, 2nd 1.88;1, 1st 3.31:1, reverse 3.33:1, final drive 4.428:1. LS and GL three-speed automatic as an option, LD five-speed manual available as an option.

BRAKES: Dual circuit, power assisted, front 9.4in discs, rear 9in drum.
TYRES: 145 x 13, 155 x 13 GLS and automatic option on LS and GL.
SUSPENSION: Front independent torsion bars with telescopic shock absorbers, rear

Instrument layout for GLS.

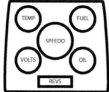

independent coil springs with telescopic shock absorbers, trailing arms.
STEERING: Rack and pinion.
DIMENSIONS: Length: 12ft 11.9in (3960mm); **width:** 5ft 6.1in (1680mm); **height:** 4ft 7.5in (1410mm); **weight:** LE/LS 2083lb (945kg), GL 2117lb (960kg), GLS 2150lb (975kg), LD 2249lb (1020kg); **turning circle:** 33.5ft (10.2m).

Talbot Sunbeam

Cars above have bumpers like those used on the Chrysler Sunbeams.

Introduced in 1979 following Peugeot's acquisition of Chrysler's European operations, the Sunbeam was discontinued in 1982. Interestingly, despite this being an original Chrysler design, the engines were in fact derivatives of Hillman engines, the 928cc from the Imp, the 1295cc and 1598cc from the Avenger.

COLOURS: Varied according to model.
ENGINES: All four-cylinder with Stromberg 150CD3 variable choke carburettor (except GLS, Ti and Lotus). LS/GL – OHC, bore 70mm, stroke 60.33mm, 928cc, maximum bhp 45 at 5600rpm. LS/GL – OHV, bore 78.6mm, stroke 66.7mm, 1295cc, maximum bhp 59 at 5000rpm. GL – OHV, bore 87.3mm, stroke 66.7mm, 1598cc, maximum bhp 69 at 4800rpm. GLS – OHV, as GL except maximum bhp 80 at 5400rpm, Stromberg 175CD3. Ti – OHV, as GL except maximum bhp 100 at 6000rpm, two Weber 40DCOE twin choke carburettors. Lotus – DOHC, 16 valve, bore 95.2mm, stroke 76.2mm, 2174cc, 150 bhp, two Dellorto DHLA45E carburettors.
GEARBOX: Four-speed, floor-mounted gear change, synchromesh on all gears. 928cc and 1295cc engine – ratios: top 1:1, 3rd 1.527:1, 2nd 2.38:1, 1st 3.89:1, reverse 4.05:1, 1598cc engine – ratios: top 1.1, 3rd 1.387:1, 2nd 2.165:1, 1st 3.538:1, reverse 3.68:1.
REAR AXLE: Semi-floating, hypoid bevel. Ratios: 928cc engine 4.375:1, 1295cc engine 3.89:1, 1598cc engine 3.54:1.
BRAKES: Dual circuit, power assisted, front 9.5in discs, rear 8in drums.
TYRES: 145 x 13 with 928cc engine, 155 x 13 with 1295/1598cc engines.
SUSPENSION: Front independent coil springs

with telescopic shock absorbers, rear four links, and coil springs with telescopic shock absorbers.
STEERING: Rack and pinion.
DIMENSIONS: Length: 12ft 6.7in (3829mm); **width:** 5ft 3.1in (1603mm); **height:** 4ft 6.9in

(1395mm); **weight:** 1.0 LS 1792lb (813kg), 1.0 GL 1808lb (820kg), 1.3 LS 1936lb (878kg), 1.3/1.6 GL 1951lb (885kg), S 1993lb (904kg).
CAPACITIES: Fuel 9 gallons (41 litres). Boot maximum 42.7ft³ (1.2m³).

Talbot Samba

Introduced in 1982, discontinued in 1986 and based on the Peugeot 104, the Samba was available as a three door hatchback and convertible with five trim options and three engines (from the Peugeot 104 and 205 range). 1982 retail price: LE 954cc £3145, a Ford Fiesta Popular Plus 957cc was £3599. Standard equipment included reversing lights, two-speed heater/blower, two-speed wipers with flick wipe, heated rear window and wash/wipe (not LE), Halogen headlights (not LE/LS), and electric front windows (GLS/Cabriolet only).

COLOURS: Varied according to model.
ENGINES: All four-cylinder, OHC with Solex 32PBISA variable choke carburettor (954 and 1124 engines). LE/LS – bore 70mm, stroke 62mm, 954cc, maximum bhp 44.5 at 6000rpm. GL – bore 72mm, stroke 69mm, 1124cc, maximum bhp 49 at 4800rpm. S/GLS – bore 75mm, stroke 77mm, 1360cc, maximum bhp 71 at 6000rpm (GLS), 79 at 5800rpm (S).
TRANSMISSION: Front-wheel drive, floor-mounted gear change, synchromesh on all gears. LE/LS/GL – four-speed gearbox. S/GLS/Cabriolet – five-speed gearbox. 954cc engine – ratios top 0.944:1, 3rd 1.377:1, 2nd 2.074:1, 1st 3.883:1, reverse 3.568:1, final drive 3.867:1. 1124cc engine – as 954cc except final drive LS 3.177, GL 3.353. 1360cc

engine ratios – top 0.904:1, 4th 1.124:1, 3rd 1.5:1, 2nd 2.296:1, 1st 3.883:1, reverse 3.568:1, final drive 3.867:1.
BRAKES: Dual circuit, front 9.5in discs, rear 7.1in drums. Power assisted on S/GLS/ Cabriolet.
TYRES: LE/LS 135 x 13, GL 145 x 13, S/GLS/ Cabriolet 165 x 70.
SUSPENSION: Front independent coil springs with telescopic shock absorbers, rear independent coil springs, trailing arms, double acting shock absorbers.
STEERING: Rack and pinion.
DIMENSIONS: Length: 11ft 6in (3506mm); **width:** 5ft 0.2in (1528mm); **height:** 4ft 5.6in (1362mm); **weight:** LE/LS/GL 1631lb (740kg), S/GLS 1742lb (790kg), Cabriolet 1874lb (850kg); **turning circle:** 30.5ft (9.3m).
CAPACITIES: Fuel 8.8 gallons (40 litres). Boot 32.75ft^3 (0.9m^3) with rear seat folded.

Note: The inclusion of the small selection of cars in this chapter, produced by Chrysler, and later Peugeot (Talbot models) after the acquisition of the Rootes Group, is to demonstrate that some Rootes names were used by these companies. Most cars featured are Talbots, due to the lack of Chrysler models that appear at car shows. Some cars even used engines derived from Rootes cars.

Chrysler/Talbot versions of vehicles originally badged as Rootes, such as Avenger, are covered in the original section, ie Hillman, and only those models produced exclusively as Chrysler/ Talbot vehicles are covered in this section.

Cars that have not been included in this chapter (due to a lack of photographs) are as follows:

Chrysler Sunbeam 1977-1978
Chrysler Horizon 1978
Talbot Horizon 1 1979-1983
Talbot Tagora 1981-1984
Talbot Solara 1 1980-1982.

In most cases some technical information has been included with the models that succeeded them.

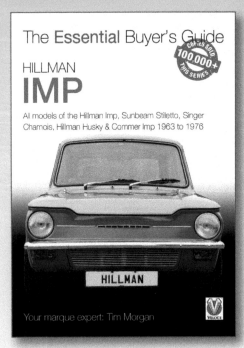
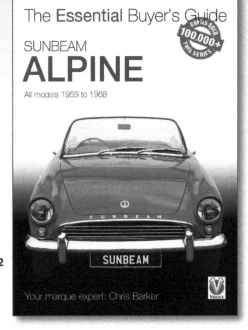

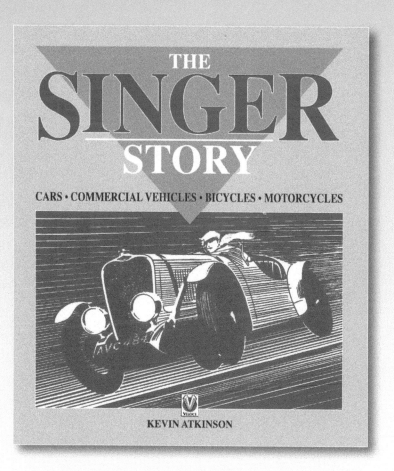

THE SINGER STORY

CARS • COMMERCIAL VEHICLES • BICYCLES • MOTORCYCLES

KEVIN ATKINSON

The Singer Story provides the definitive history of one of Britain's oldest and most important and influential car manufacturers. Thoroughly researched and with over 300 photos this is an important piece of automotive history.

ISBN: 978-1-845849-66-5
Available as an Ebook
300+ b&w pictures

• email: info@veloce.co.uk • Tel: +44(0)1305 260068

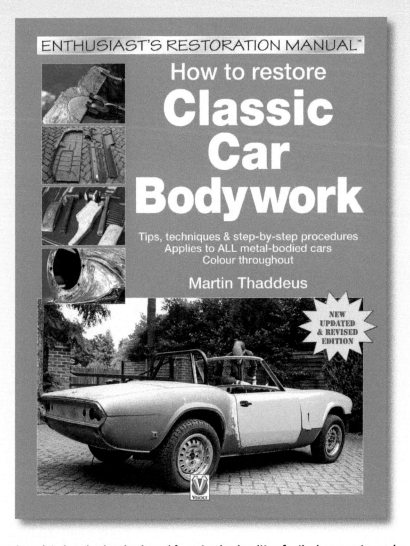

ENTHUSIAST'S RESTORATION MANUAL™

How to restore
Classic
Car
Bodywork

Tips, techniques & step-by-step procedures
Applies to ALL metal-bodied cars
Colour throughout

Martin Thaddeus

NEW
UPDATED
& REVISED
EDITION

VELOCE

Now in updated, revised and enlarged format, a book written for the home restorer who, until now, lacked the confidence to tackle bodywork. With specially devised techniques which don't rely on workshop plant, this work spans the gap between professional and amateur. The text is readable, the photos bright and the instruction clear. A real boon for the enthusiast.

ISBN: 978-1-787111-67-7
Paperback • 27x20.7cm • 128 pages • 350 colour pictures

For more info on Veloce titles, visit our website at www.veloce.co.uk

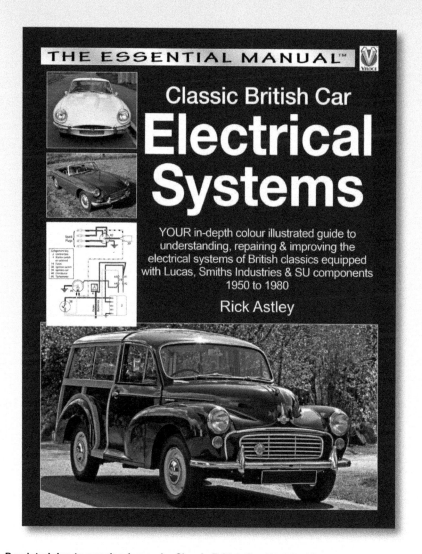

THE ESSENTIAL MANUAL™

Classic British Car
Electrical
Systems

YOUR in-depth colour illustrated guide to
understanding, repairing & improving the
electrical systems of British classics equipped
with Lucas, Smiths Industries & SU components
1950 to 1980

Rick Astley

Reprinted due to popular demand – *Classic British Car Electrical Systems* provides the
theory, component parts, and full system operating explanations for each major electrical
system used from 1950 to 1980, with particular emphasis on Lucas, Smith and SU
components that were ubiquitous in British cars of the period.

ISBN: 978-1-845849-48-1
Paperback • 27x20.7cm • 192 pages • 419 pictures

• email: info@veloce.co.uk • Tel: +44(0)1305 260068

Index

Hillman

Humber

Chrysler/Talbot